ETIQUETTE FOR THE CHRIST SCHOOL GENTLEMAN

Printed for the Office of Student Life
Christ School
Arden, N.C.

ISBN 0-9703041-5-3

First Edition 2005

ACKNOWLEDGEMENTS

Most of the material in this book is not new. It is a compilation and an assimilation of information drawn from several sources on the subject. Christ School gratefully acknowledges that the material in this book has been previously published in Hampden Sydney College's own guide to etiquette entitled *To Manner Born, To Manners Bred*, and in Jane Hight McMurry's books entitled *The Etiquette Advantage®* and *The Dance Steps of Life*. It has, herein, been adapted for our own use and slightly edited for this publication. Reprinted with permission. All rights are reserved.

We thank the contributing authors for allowing us to utilize their material and to share their knowledge on this subject with the young men at Christ School.

Emily Post's Etiquette is also recognized as a standard of good etiquette in this country and it, too, has been a guide in writing this book.

If the reader would like to reference the above material in its entirety please refer to the Reference page in the back of this book for bibliographic information to locate these books and references.

FOREWARD

Christ School's mission is to produce educated men of good character, prepared for both scholastic achievement in college and productive citizenship in adult society. Along the way, we strive to help our students be *The Best a Boy Can Be*- a motto we've adopted which is embraced in our four-fold philosophy emphasizing academics, spiritual growth, athletics, and a community service work program. We, therefore, expect our students to become men of good moral character, who cultivate tolerance, civility and respect for others, who are, in turn, respected by others and who are good citizens in their communities and society as a whole.

This book is about etiquette- the code of good form for decency in behavior and conformity to acceptable standards in a civilized world. When primitive families originally came together to form tribes, they established certain norms of behavior to maintain order, protect the rights of others and to avoid tension and conflict. As communities of people continued to grow, etiquette evolved into the elaborate, formal and carefully prescribed forms of behavior associated with the courts of monarchs who embodied the power of the nation.

Today, while we live in a less formal culture and are not concerned with the proper way to behave at a royal court, there are still certain practices or norms that are expected in our civilized society in order to co-exist with many people. The need to respect the rights of others, to reduce tensions and to avoid conflict has never been greater than it is today. Although the protocol of good manners may have changed slightly over time, the timelessness of civility and etiquette endures.

Your first steps into the social and business world may not be easy. Prospective employers may ask you to lunch, to cocktails or to dinner. They might even ask to come to your home to see how you live. How you handle yourself on those social occasions will likely influence whether or not you are offered a job. It will undoubtedly also have an influence on what opportunities you will have in life and what doors may (or may not) be opened to you.

This book of etiquette is meant to give you this exposure and an awareness that others might never achieve. The information inside, is offered in the hope that, if you have missed acquiring it along the way, that you will now find it useful and be able to apply it to your own advantage. Although good manners can offer a finishing touch which give a man an edge in life, they must be combined with common decency, respect for others, honor and integrity for you to truly be *The Best a Boy Can Be*.

CONTENTS

CHAPTER 1:

MEETING & GREETING

IT IS A FRIENDLY PRACTICE IN THIS COUNTRY to acknowledge or speak to everyone you meet or pass. Speak a person's name if you know it and say "Hi" or "Hello, "Good Morning," "What's Happening" or any other friendly greeting. What's important is that you do not fail to acknowledge each other.

Meeting and greeting by both men and women typically includes smiling, making eye contact, saying hello and standing up to shake hands. Years ago, a woman stood only to meet and greet an older woman or dignitary. A woman also did not shake hands unless she chose to extend her hand to a man. Today, equal respect is shown to both sexes. Always extend your hand immediately upon meeting people for the first time, look them straight in the eyes, smile and say "Hello" in a friendly manner.

Smile
The best way to make others (and yourself) feel good is to smile while looking at them. Smiling puts others at ease, shows you care about them and relieves tension that might exist.

Eye Contact
Look people directly in the eye when you greet them. Looking directly at them develops a sense of trust. You should not dwell on this point of contact and stare into their eyes for too long a time but it is important to stay focused on the person you are speaking with and not to let your

eyes roam or be distracted. After making good eye contact, keep looking at the person's total face for five seconds, then each part for a few seconds (eyes, nose, forehead, chin, etc.) This helps ease the eye contact but keeps your eyes from roaming elsewhere or becoming distracted.

Shaking Hands

It is correct for either a man or a woman to initiate a handshake. You are judged by your handshake so a warm and sincere handshake makes a positive connection with the other person. Shake hands firmly (but carefully if wearing rings–it can be painful with too firm a squeeze).

A handshake with no tension or tone in the hand feels weak and lifeless and is called a limp fish handshake. It can be interpreted as wimpy or lacking self confidence. The bone crusher handshake exerts so much strength that it hurts and sends a message of aggressiveness, insecurity or bullying and insensitivity The fingertip extender shake conveys a message of weakness and lacking self confidence. The gloved handshake (also called the preacher handshake) conveys the message of comfort and consolation. It is given by shaking hands with the right hand and then placing the left hand on top of the clasped hands. It is best used with close friends or when conveying sympathy or offering comfort. It should not be used as an everyday greeting.

Make your handshake simply firm and warm- lasting for two to three seconds or shakes of the hand. When you meet someone you know at a social function, it is not necessary to shake hands, but it is usual if you have not seen him or her for some time. Encounters with those you know well or see often do not require a handshake, but never ignore an outstretched hand or hesitate to extend your own if you are comfortable doing so.

Hello

Greet others with a friendly "hello" and be enthusiastic. "How are you" is an overused greeting that can sound mechanical and evoke an even more mechanical "Fine, how are you?" Don't ask a person how he is unless you truly want to know. Other positive greetings like "It's nice to meet you, I've heard a lot about you from my roommate," or "I hear you play on your school's lacrosse team," are upbeat and will likely lead to conversations both of you will enjoy.

Standing

Modern manners encourage both women and men to rise for all introductions. Standing to meet someone is a gesture of self-respect and respect to those in attendance. A man stands when a woman enters the room for the first time and continues to stand until the woman is seated or leaves the area. A man stands when a woman comes to sit by him. The man *sits* after the woman is seated. A man stands when a woman leaves. (Note: The man stands for every woman who enters his area and stops to talk. He does not need to rise for unknown women who are simply passing through his area. The man completely stands if the woman stops to talk. He does not sit until the woman sits or leaves.)

Women and men should rise when a guest enters the room. It is good manners to offer a guest a seat and to remain standing until the guest is seated. The host should stand when the guest rises to leave and remains standing as long as the guest stands and then walks the guest to the door, the elevator, his car, etc. Business protocol does not require that business people rise for assistants or secretaries who frequently enter and exit the room.

Introductions

The most important part of meeting and greeting is called the introduction. A good introduction can put everyone at ease. A poor introduction or no introduction at all, makes an uncomfortable situation for everyone in a group. We've all been in that awkward situation when we encounter an individual we know who is with someone we don't know. We talk for a moment and the unknown person stands there uncomfortably. When no move by either party is made to introduce the stranger, we leave the encounter feeling uncomfortable and a bit guilty. The stranger leaves the encounter feeling unfulfilled and hurt. The outward appearance was that he wasn't important enough to either party to be acknowledged. The real reason the friend might have neglected to introduce him is his feeling of insecurity about how to make a correct introduction.

When you are with another person, always introduce that person to friends and acquaintances you meet whether on campus or anywhere else. In addition, if you come upon a friend, an individual or a group of people you don't know or who may not know you, make the first move and introduce yourself. If you are wearing a cap, it would be polite to remove it. If you are wearing gloves, remove the one from the hand you extend. If removing a glove is not feasible, simply say "Please excuse my glove". (White gloves worn at a formal affair with full dress attire are not removed or apologized for).

How to Introduce Yourself
Always rise for any introduction. Rising is a gesture of respect for both the person to whom you are being introduced and yourself. Stand up, look the person in the eye, extend your hand for a firm handshake and say your name and something about yourself. For example, *"Hello, I'm Duffy Davenport. I'm Simms Davenport's brother from Wilmington."*

The key is to give as much concise information about yourself as possible in a short amount of time. This is conversation bait. Conversation bait encourages the other person to respond to the information (*"It's nice to meet you Duffy. I know Simms and his roommate Hal. I've heard them tell stories about you when you were at Christ School..."*).

How to Properly Introduce Others
Stand up and make eye contact as you are saying each person's name.

Say the older, more important or female's name first followed by one of the following phrases: "I'd like to present to you... ", "I would like to introduce to you...", "I would like for you to meet...", or simply "this is..." followed by the name of the person being introduced. For example, "Grandy, I'd like for you to meet my friend Reed Cluxton."

Make each person feel important by providing specific information about each of them as you make the introduction. Telling about the interests, special talents, hometowns or even the schools of the people being introduced will give a basis for conversation. For example, say, "Mr. Krieger, I'd like to introduce to you my friend from camp, Matt, who is a magician from Barbados." An introduction such as this can result in several avenues of conversation – camp experience, magic and exciting places like Barbados!

Three Rules for Making Proper Social Introductions

- Introduce less important persons *to* more important persons.
- Men *to* women
- Younger people *to* older people (Accomplish this by saying the more important woman's or older person's name first.)
- *Exceptions:* Outsiders are given precedence when being introduced to a family member. The exception is a child introducing his mother or father. Women are presented to ambassadors, chiefs of state, royalty and dignitaries of the church.

Example of Introducing a Parent and a Young Friend

"Mom, I'd like to introduce *to you* my friend, Eleanor Cooper. Eleanor, this is my mom, Mrs. Davenport, who made the cookies for our trip to the Bahamas."

"Dad, I would like to introduce *to you* my friend, Pat Halligan who was in Jay's class in New Hampshire. Pat, this is my father, Mr. Talbert."

Examples of Introductions to Church and Government Officials

"Bishop Daniels, I'd like to introduce *to you* my friend, Mary Spinx. She serves on the vestry at The Chapel of the Cross in Chapel Hill."

"Mr. President, may I present Worth Price, a Vice President at Allied Pharmaceutical."

Example of Introducing a Teacher and a Parent

(Even if your teacher is younger than your parents, show deference and respect to the teacher by making the teacher the most important person in the way you phrase the introduction.)

"Ms. Barry, I'd like to introduce to you my mother, Jane McMurry. Mom, this is my math teacher, Ms. Barry."

Example of Family Introductions

"Elsa DeLoach, I'd like to introduce my brother, Jackson Brown."

Examples of Introducing Two Friends to Each Other (one male and one female)
"Nancy Avery, I'd like to introduce Tom Pappas. Tom, I met Nancy this summer at the Yacht Club. Nancy, Tom is the friend I told you about who has the house on the lake in New Hampshire." (Provide something of interest to talk about.)

Polish your introductions by practicing the following:

- **Introduce a less important person to a more important person** if you can determine the more important person. Do this by first saying the more important person's name. For example,

    "Mr. President, I'd like to present *to you* my uncle, Governor Nutting."
    Or, "Professor Stimey, I'd like to introduce to you my roommate from Virginia, Karen Layman."

- **Introduce a man to a woman when they are the same age.** Do this by first saying the woman's name. For example,

    "Ellen Carter, I'd like to introduce to you our new classmate, Howard Allen. Howard, Ellen is my cousin from Pennsylvania."

- **Introduce a younger person to an older person.** Do this by first saying the older person's name. For example,

    "Grandmother, I'd like to introduce to you my guitar teacher, Ms. Poole. Ms. Poole, this is my grandmother from Allendale, Mrs. Talbert."

- **Introduce a new friend to a group.** Do this by first saying the new friend's name. For example,

    "Linda McMurry, I'd like you to meet my friends." Then say the names of the members in the group or have your friends introduce themselves to your friend.

Note: There isn't always a right or a wrong way to make the introduction so don't let that scare you out of introducing people. The more important thing is to be sure and introduce people.

<u>Responding to Introductions</u>
- Do not reply with a simple "Hi," or "Hello."
- Stand up, extend your hand, smile, lean toward the person and say, "Hello, David". How do you do" Some people prefer to say the phrase "It's nice to meet you." Even though the traditional response is "How do you do," remember it's helpful if you can personalize what you say.
- Always repeat the person's name .
- Immediately ask the person to repeat a name if you didn't hear the name properly or are not sure of how to pronounce it.

VISITORS

Whenever you encounter a stranger on campus, introduce yourself and ask if you can be of help. Remember that every individual or group visiting the Christ School campus for any reason is a guest of the school and, as such, should be treated with courtesy. Also remember that whenever you are on another campus you are a representative of this school and should behave as if Christ School's reputation depended on your actions – for it does.

INTERVIEWING

If there is ever a time to put on your best clothes and your best manners, it is when you go for an interview. This is primarily true for a job interview but it also applies to other interviews as well. When you write to request the interview, you should do so on good stationery. The resumé you enclose must be prepared carefully. When you write to thank the interviewer for his or her time, you should also do so on good stationery and in your very best handwriting style. You do not want your appearance and conduct at the interview to be anything less than the best.

Have your hair trimmed and neat, your nails clean and your shoes shined. Find out the accepted standard of business dress where you are applying and choose your wardrobe to meet that standard. It is important to look as if you belong. Whether it is a suit, white shirt and tie (banks, brokerage houses, sales positions) or a sports jacket, dress trousers, button-down shirt and tie (high tech firms, service industries), choose carefully and tastefully and wear the best you have.

Shake hands firmly and look the interviewer in the eyes. Start by answering the simple questions that are asked, but as you get comfortable with your interviewer, open up, expand on answers and ask questions.

What you gain at the interview can be lost at a meal or social event that follows if you fail to use proper etiquette. Employers want someone who can do the job in the office and can represent them well outside of the office and they will judge prospective employees on both skills. Know and follow the rules of traditional etiquette; they are your best guide. But, if you make a mistake, apologize, if necessary, or be secure enough to laugh at your own gaff and move on. Always remember that your manners *will* make a difference.

WOMEN IN BUSINESS

The person who interviews you, hires you and supervises you is as likely to be a woman as a man. In the future, a great many of your professional colleagues will be women. In a work environment you will deal with women and men who are in rank superior, equal and inferior to you, every one of whom should be treated with respect for the contribution she or he makes to the organization.

In a professional setting courtesy never is abandoned, but some of the traditional social courtesies of men toward women are. You would not rise from your chair if a female co-worker or a female secretary enters your office (if you are lucky enough to have an office.) However, you would stand up when your superior — whether female or male-enters your office (until such time as it is made clear that this is not expected), and you would always rise to greet any client or visitor of either sex.

In a traditional social setting, a man does not extend his hand to a woman. It is her prerogative to initiate the handshake. However, in a business setting this standard form of greeting may be initiated by anyone. It is a small, but important, recognition of equality. If you wish to revert to the traditional approach on social occasions, especially with older women, that is fine, but switching back and forth may get a bit confusing.

You would not stand up when a woman enters a meeting room or help her with her chair at the conference table. You would not hold a door open so that she can precede you through it, although you should never let a door slam in anyone's face. You would not offer to do something for a female colleague on the assumption that she cannot do it for herself, but you should never refuse a request for help or ignore a situation in which any colleague is struggling; even then, ask first.

When a group from the office goes out to lunch or perhaps elsewhere after work, is this a social situation or an extension of the work environment? If there is no significant break in time, consider it an extension of the work day. Treat your female colleagues as you would in the office. If, however, you are invited with office colleagues to dinner, which is obviously a separate social occasion, then it is time to put on your party clothes and party manners.

SPECIAL COURTESIES TOWARD WOMEN

The many special courtesies which men were once taught to extend to women, and ladies were taught to expect from gentlemen, are not often practiced today. The exceptional treatment of women was motivated by two contradictory ideas. The first was that women hold a unique and important place in society and *deserve* special treatment. The second was that women are inferior and *need* special treatment.

The best advice is to develop in your dealings with others an attitude which puts their needs and comfort ahead of your own and to act accordingly. However, on traditional social occasions the following basic courtesies should be extended to women of all ages:

- Do not precede a woman through a doorway, unless it is necessary to light or clear the way. If a door is closed, it should be opened for a woman; this includes a car door.
- As mentioned previously, stand up when a woman (or an older man) enters a room or approaches to greet you. Never remain seated while a woman stands unless she asks you to do so.
- When a woman drops an item, lean over and retrieve it for her.
- Assist a woman with her chair at meals.

CHAPTER 2:

DRESS

THE SCOTTISH TARTAN NAMES THE CLAN, the shoe reflects the athlete's sport and the uniform reflects occupation, rank or military service branch. Once upon a time, kings banned non-royalty from wearing specific clothing styles and rich fabrics. Corduroy was literally the cloth of kings. In today's non-fairy tale times, modern standards of acceptability require certain attire in private clubs, private schools, business and athletic competitions. To go against the unofficial laws of dress won't result in a king-decreed death today, but it certainly can result in loss of privileges and/or doors closed to great opportunities in life. The socially smart individual investigates and learns the rules of the game.

People who fit in, are well received and are generally accepted by members of their group, typically wear clothes that are acceptable for the occasion and the venue. Students who fit in, wear clothes acceptable to their friends and teachers. Well-informed travelers wear clothing acceptable to the countries they visit. For example, Arab countries require women in public to completely cover their bodies, so a bikini in Saudi Arabia would be inexcusable.

The outcast often becomes the person who does not dress in clothing acceptable to the members of the group he/she may be a part of. In fact, that individual sends the non-verbal message that he/she rejects that group. On some occasions, creative clothing is an acceptable expression of individuality, but generally, it should be an exception to the rule and not the rule, if an individual wants to be taken seriously and be respected by others.

The primary consideration when choosing clothes is that others will be looking at you more than you will be looking at yourself. Think about how people make each other feel when they look at each other. Good? Grossed out? Disgusted? Embarrassed? Good manners mean making others feel at ease and most people feel at ease when they and others around them fit in. Polite people take time to present themselves in a way that is pleasing to others.

Style versus Fashion

Style, or "the quality of imagination and individuality, expressed in one's activities and tasks," belongs to you. Fashion, which is "something that is the current trend," belongs to others. You can develop your own style and if you choose to, can adhere to it all of your life. Chasing the latest fashion is time-consuming and expensive; and in fact, you can never capture it for long for the nature of fashion is constant change. Developing your own style begins with knowing who you are. What you wear tells other people something about you. As you get older and wiser, there will be more and more times when you will very much want it to say what is appropriate.

Quality and Tradition

Quality in your clothing is important. It is not always synonymous with cost but is made into a garment, not bestowed upon it by the attachment of a designer's logo. How much quality can you afford? That is a decision which only you can make, but here are some suggestions:

When it counts, stretch to get the best. A good suit for job interviews (or high quality sports jacket and slacks) is a good investment and will last well into your professional life.

Limit the quantity. You may have dozens of jeans and even more T-shirts and sweatshirts to wear to class, but you don't need dozens of suits and sports jackets. A few well-chosen items should meet your needs.

Shop smart. Everything is on sale or sold at discount some time in some place.

Don't forget your birthday, Christmas, Hanukkah, etc. Ask for gift certificates if you would rather not trust Great Aunt Gertrude's taste in ties; but if you need a few nice clothes, this is a good way to get them.

Spend for the best effect. You may not have been able to afford the most expensive navy blue blazer, but you probably can afford a really striking tie.

Take some time, think about what you need; look around and spend wisely. Also, rely on tradition. Men's business, semi-formal and formal social attire has changed very little over the years. When you own the company you can set the dress code. When you are trying to get your first job, you should find out what the standards are and conform to them. In most cases, those standards will be traditional ones.

Traditional clothing usually means natural fabrics. Natural fabrics are good value because most wear for a very long time. Natural fabrics, however, require greater–usually professional–care. The positive impression made by a freshly laundered, well-pressed shirt is worth the effort.

Clothing need not be made of 100% natural fabric. Blending in synthetic fibers has produced clothing more suitable for travel or more desirable if you have to spend a good deal of time driving, but fabrics which are made entirely or mostly of such fibers as virgin wool and long-staple cotton will have a feel, appearance and durability which is unequaled. However, there are problems with natural fabrics–pure linen will always be wrinkled, recycled wool is 100% natural but is often coarse and scratchy against the skin; and it may be difficult to get spots out of silk. There is no need to pay the price of camel hair and cashmere. Look at the other label on the garment–not the one which tells you the price, the one that tells you the content; it is the better guide to value.

Remember that following tradition is the best–and safest–substitute for a yet uncertain style. What follows represents a traditional approach to social and business attire. It is a "getting started" guide, not holy writ.

Casual or Informal: Sports Jacket and Slacks

Casual never means uncoordinated, disheveled, un-ironed or dirty. It means rather that you wear your sports jacket, blazer or sweater with a sports or dress shirt open at the neck, or a knit shirt, opened or buttoned at the neck, or a turtleneck, or some combination of these if you want to layer.

Casual trousers, except jeans, should be creased if worn with a jacket or blazer and tie. Jeans and lightweight cotton trousers should always be clean and reasonably smooth, although not necessarily pressed. These are best worn with a shirt (knit or woven) open at the neck and/or a sweater, but can be worn with a blazer or sports jacket if the event is decidedly casual. This is also true of a sweater worn with only a T-shirt under it. You need to tread cautiously here. If you arrive at a party and are the only one wearing a tie, you can take it off and open your shirt collar. If you arrive at a party in jeans and sweater with no shirt, and every other male guest has a jacket and tie, it is too late to remedy the situation. Of course it is fair to ask here, "Why do I have to dress like everyone else?" It is not a question of dressing like everyone else; it is a matter of dressing appropriately for the occasion and meeting the expectations of your hosts. Within the bounds of what is appropriate, you may be as individual as possible.

In warm weather, shorts may be substituted for jeans or lightweight cotton trousers and worn with shirt (knit or woven, long-sleeved or short) open at the neck and/or a sweater. Casual shorts are not usually worn with a jacket and tie.

If you choose a sports shirt instead of a dress shirt, it is best to choose those which are plain, checked, or muted plaid. Very bold patterns and colors are tricky to coordinate with patterned sports jackets. They will often work well with a blue blazer or plain sweater. Be very careful when mixing patterns. Remember Beau Brumell's rule, "Never wear checks and stripes."

A striped, pastel, or finely patterned dress shirt with a tie is appropriate for casual wear.

Semiformal: The Suit

The virtues most highly prized in a man's suit are the quality of the fabric and the care in tailoring. Through college, you may need only one suit. Purchase the best you can afford and take care of it. The most useful and versatile suits are dark solids, muted plaids, or fine stripes on dark backgrounds in gray and blue. Brown or earth tone suits are fine for day wear but are not appropriate for evening. Gray and blue work all day. The best buy is an all season or tropical weight worsted wool. With an overcoat, it will serve outside on the coldest day, and with air conditioning, it will serve inside on the hottest. If you want a suit for summer, the most useful are poplins in solid colors—usually tan, olive, or navy. The fabric of these suits almost always is a cotton-synthetic blend to help them hold their shape. In summer, lighter colored and earth tone suits may be worn in the evening, although not to a formal occasion. You can make your suit more versatile by varying your shirts and ties—pastel Oxford cloth button-down with a bright regimental tie for day and a white broadcloth straight or tab collar with a small pattern tie for evening. If you want a more contemporary look for day wear, a dark shirt and tie will work.

Single-breasted suits have two or three front buttons—either is fine. Double-breasted suits are equally acceptable, but you will probably not find them as comfortable to wear since they should always be fully buttoned. If you have just one suit, single breasted is better. When you buy or wear a vest, be sure that it covers your belt and the waistband of your trousers. Whether or not you cuff your trousers is also a matter of personal taste. Cuffs give a nice finish to the trousers of business suits, but suits with trousers that are not cuffed are considered dressier. The trousers of a tuxedo, for example, are never cuffed.

Be careful when it comes to designer suits. They are usually expensive, but more importantly, the cut is often non-traditional. The designer is trying to be unique. There is nothing wrong with a nontraditional cut if it fits and flatters you as well as it does the professional model in the advertisement; if you look that good, go for it.

Suits should be worn with dress shirts and ties. Shirts with the collar open, knit shirts and turtlenecks are worn with blazers, sports coats and sweaters. If your company has a "dress down" day, don't try to dress down a suit. Leave it at home and go casual.

The Blazer

There is no more versatile and essential item in your wardrobe than the navy blue blazer. It may be worn on most occasions. Black is almost as good but will never look as informal for day wear. Earth tones—even expensive camel hair blazers—never look as smart at night. The navy blazer does it all. Khaki trousers dress it down; grey wool trousers dress it up. It will go with just about any shirt or tie. The most useful fabric is an all-season worsted wool. If you choose a heavier wool flannel you will need another blazer for summer. A navy linen blend is good, or in summer, you can go into the lighter color solids. Traditional blazers have two or three front buttons—either is fine. Double-breasted blazers are less comfortable to wear and are more formal.

If you want to personalize your navy blazer, consider buttons with a College seal, or your initials, or other decorative brass or gold buttons. These can be expensive, but when the blazer has worn out, you can transfer the buttons to a new one.

The Sports Jacket

Another jacket that can be almost as versatile as a navy blazer is a sports jacket. Choose a subdued pattern in shades of blue or gray if you plan to use it for both day and evening wear. Sports jackets are usually of heavier fabrics than blazers and therefore a wool sports jacket will not carry you through the summer. Plan to have a summer weight jacket, unless you have no need of a jacket during the summer months. Again, like the blazer, casual cotton trousers dress it down; creased wool trousers dress it up. Since sports jackets are usually patterned, shirts and ties are more restricted. White is always safe, as are solid colors that pick up or complement the colors in the jacket. Solid color ties, regimental stripes, and fine patterns will work, but again care should be taken when mixing patterns.

Shirts

There is no end to the variety of colors and styles of dress shirts. White works with everything and goes anywhere. You do, however, need to vary the style—an Oxford cloth button down with a casual outfit, a straight collar broadcloth with a suit in the evening. These terms, by the way, refer to the way the fabric—usually all cotton or cotton blend—is woven. Oxford cloth, heavier to the hand and thicker to the eye, is considered the less formal of the two; broadcloth, which feels smoother and looks thinner, is considered the more formal of the two. For example, you would never find a full-dress shirt in Oxford cloth. Also, because broadcloth is thin, it is best to wear a white T-shirt under it. These fabrics can be made into any style of shirt, although button-down

HOW TO TIE A TIE

Well-dressed men know how to tie bow and neckties correctly. Follow these simple diagrams and you will quickly master techniques for tying a tie.

How to Tie a Bow Tie

- Start with one end about one and one-half inches below the other and bring the long end through the center.
- Form a loop with the short end and center it where the knot will.
- Bring the long end over it.
- Form a loop with the long end and push it through the knot behind the front loop.
- Adjust the ends slowly so that they are about the same on either side of the knot.

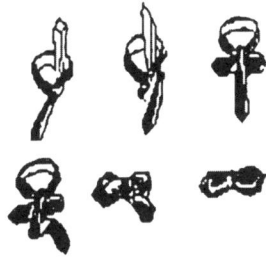

Note: If after six tries you can't make it, take a break and call Mr. Cluxton!

How to Tie a Half Windsor Knot

- Place the tie around your neck with the wider end hanging on the right side of your chest about twelve inches below the narrow end which is hanging over the left side of your chest.
- Cross the wide end over the narrow end and pull it around and underneath the narrow end.
- Carry the wide end up through the loop and pass it around the front from left to right.
- Bring the wide end through the loop again and pass it through the knot in front.
- Tighten the knot slowly as you draw it up to the collar.

How to Tie a Four-in-Hand Knot

- Place the tie around your neck with the wider end hanging on the right side of your chest about twelve inches below the narrow end which is hanging over the left side of your chest.
- Cross the wide end over the narrow end and pull it up through the loop.
- Hold the front of the knot loosely with the index finger and pull the wide end through the loop in front.
- Tighten the knot slowly while holding the narrow end and sliding the knot to the collar.

collar shirts are usually of the less formal Oxford cloth. The cuffs may be button—appropriate at all times—or French which require cuff-links and are dressier. The collar style—straight, Windsor, pinned, tab, etc.—is largely up to you; but button-down collars, even on white shirts, should not be worn with a suit to a semiformal event at night. However, if you are going to wear a shirt with the collar open to a casual party the button-down is the best choice. Tab and pin-collar shirts should not be worn without a tie.

Although many businesses have abandoned the "only white shirts" requirement, white is always appropriate and gives you fewer coordination problems. Pale blue is the next best. If you do wear colored, striped or patterned shirts in a business or semiformal social environment, keep the suit solid and the tie solid or the pattern subtle. Knit shirts with collars – long or short sleeved- and turtlenecks may be worn for casual wear with blazers and sports jackets. They are best not worn with suits. T-shirts are underwear and should not be worn without a shirt or sweater at most social functions.

Formal: Black Tie

"Black tie" refers to a dinner jacket (tuxedo), a garment made popular by King Edward VII. It replaced "white tie," the full dress tail coat, at events which the Victorians and Edwardians considered less formal. Black is always proper. Choose a traditional styling—shawl collar, notched collar, or double breasted. The shawl collared jacket is traditionally worn with a cummerbund and the notched-collared jacket with a black satin vest. The double-breasted jacket requires neither cummerbund nor vest, but must be kept buttoned. White dinner jackets are worn only in the summer.

Also avoid colored shirts, ruffles, lace and large jewelry. Formal attire is "black tie" and therefore, requires one. Shun the trend of tie-less formal attire. There is a reason why men are supposed to look so "dull" in formal wear; it is to allow women to shine in all their splendid finery. On these occasions, you are not to be the center of attention.

However, you do have some room for personal expression. Dress trousers made from a family tartan can be striking. They should be without cuffs and have the same black satin stripe as other formal trousers. If you wear a tartan, you should have a legitimate family claim to it no matter how remote. Vests and cummerbunds, but not ties, can be patterned. Beautiful ones can be purchased. Seek out something which is important to you–a family tartan, an ethnic or cultural design, fraternity colors, etc.

Shoes are always black and should be highly polished if not of patent leather. If you do not have formal attire, you may rent one from a reliable supplier, but the cost is such that if you have frequent need for formal wear, you should consider buying.

White Tie

Few people own full dress. This too can be rented. Remember that the guest's tie and vest are white. The man wearing the tailcoat with the black vest and tie is the butler.

If you can not rent a dinner jacket when it is required, a dark suit, and only a dark suit, will do. Choose navy or black or the darkest solid gray you own. Wear a white shirt with a straight collar and French cuffs, if you have one, and a dark but, ironically, not black, silk bow tie, and you will blend right in. If you cannot rent full dress when it is required, a dinner jacket will do.

Accessories

Most of your **neckties** should be of silk in fine overall patterns, regimental stripes, or solids; these are the most versatile. Bow ties–self-tie or pre-tied (not clip-on) work as well as long ties. It is your choice. Ties are also made of fine wool for winter or cotton for summer. Good neckties are expensive, but you really don't need a great many and this is a good item to pick up on sale. You can even get by with one tie–your college tie, either stripe or shield. A college tie can be worn anytime and anywhere you wear a suit or blazer or, if the colors work, with a sports jacket. It is like a uniform, always correct, never out of fashion. Wear it often and always with pride.

When choosing a **belt,** dark belts are generally more practical and should typically match the color of the leather shoes with which they are worn. Cloth belts are for casual wear. Choose buckles that do not attract attention.

Men have traditionally worn little or no **jewelry** such as wrist watches or perhaps a signet ring or wedding band. Today, some men choose to wear necklaces, bracelets, and sometimes, even an earring. Although this is a matter of personal taste, less is usually better. When wearing jewelry (watch, ring, cufflinks, tie clasp) it should be of the same metal tone – gold, silver or stainless steel for watches. In a formal business environment (i.e., suit and tie), such items should not be worn. In a more casual business environment or in an informal social environment, it is your choice to do so if that is your style; but you should stick to simple gold or silver pieces. Traditionally, men do not wear cut gemstones–those that sparkle. They might wear cabochon-polished-gemstones or semi-precious stones such as onyx or carnelians. If you choose to wear and can afford a gemstone, it is most appropriate to choose your birthstone.

Keep the top outside **pocket** of a jacket neat–avoid having pens and handkerchiefs inside and poking out. The best place for a wallet, pens and pencils is in the inside jacket pocket–not the pocket of your trousers. It is also handy to carry a handkerchief in your inside pocket. A final piece of advice about pockets is to keep your hands out of them. A man with his hands thrust into his pockets appears insecure and is not readily able to shake hands with others.

If your attire includes a **vest**, leave the lowest button unbuttoned.

Socks worn with a suit should as closely as possible match the color of the suit and be long enough (over-the-calf) to prevent a break between the top of your sock and the cuff of your trousers when you sit down. With casual outfits, you can be more adventurous with colors and patterns-or sometimes in the summer, sockless - but the color of your socks should always have some relation to the color of your shoes and trousers, not to your shirt or tie. Generally, dark socks should be worn with dress shoes.

Shoes worn with a suit or dress trousers should be dark, of smooth leather and well polished. Cordovan is the most versatile color. Black shoes should not be worn with brown suits or trousers, nor brown shoes with gray or blue. Cordovan goes with all colors. Lace-up shoes are more formal than slip-ons, but a dressy pair of slip-ons will satisfy most needs. Penny loafers, moccasin-type shoes and any shoes of a leather that is not polished, are for casual wear. Athletic shoes can be worn with jeans to a casual social function, but be sure that the event is really that casual. Sandals, too, are for very casual social occasions. White socks are usually worn only with athletic shoes and never with sandals.

Hats

There are those who believe that hat etiquette should be more relaxed and modernized. However, to try to anticipate all instances or settings in which more relaxed rules might be acceptable would be impossible. Therefore, it would be wise to follow the basic hat rules of our time which say that today's gentleman shows respect for others by remembering the following pointers.

- *He removes his hat when being introduced or saying good-bye.*
- *He removes his hat while talking with a woman, an older man, or any person he wishes to show special respect.*
- *He raises his hat in recognition of a friend when passing and removes his hat completely in the presence of an assembly of friends.*
- *He removes his hat with his left hand leaving his right hand free to shake hands—or removes with right and transfers to the left hand.*
- *He tips his hat to an acquainted woman he meets on the street and removes it completely when speaking to her. He may replace his hat if he and the woman walk ahead together.*
- *He removes his hat inside most buildings.*
- *He removes his hat and stands for the national anthem.*
- *He removes his hat when he says the pledge of allegiance and when the American flag passes in a parade,*
- *He removes his hat in an apartment-house or hotel elevator.*
- *He removes his hat at solemn outdoor ceremonies such as a burial.*
- *He refrains from wearing hats, caps, toboggans, do-rags or other head dress in public (including radical hairstyles) that could leave an unfavorable impression on others. (An exception to this would be on Halloween or other purposefully costumed occasions.) When in doubt, ask an adult whose opinion you trust.*
- *A man does not remove his hat in Orthodox Jewish synagogues and some Conservative synagogues, stores, lobbies, corridors, and elevators of public buildings such as stations and post offices.*

It is important to remember that the visor of your cap hides your eyes, especially if you have a tendency to drop your head slightly when you meet or talk with someone. Losing eye contact with someone to whom you are being introduced or with whom you are talking diminishes the effectiveness of the contact and may even be taken as an indication that you have no interest or wish to end the contact. It is therefore, a good idea to remove your cap when meeting someone for the first time or when having an extended or serious conversation.

Gloves

The custom of wearing gloves is very old. When to leave on gloves and when to remove them hinges on customs of the past. Gloves originally were worn for protection from cold weather and from the danger of battle, and today, people still wear gloves for protection, warmth and fashion. Knights removed their gauntlets to offer bare and vulnerable hands as a sign of friendship and as an act of faith. If you are wearing gloves and you are introduced to someone who is not, remove your gloves to shake hands. Men also remove gloves when shaking hands with women. The man may leave his gloves on without apologizing if it is too awkward and time consuming to remove his gloves. Men remove gloves when inside buildings unless the gloves are part of a wedding ensemble or dress for a fancy ball. And today, as in the age of knights, men always remove gloves when eating.

Handkerchiefs

Handkerchiefs need not be worn as an adornment to a man's coat pocket. They can come in handy, however, for a number of uses when a man becomes accustomed to the convenience of having one tucked away in an inside coat pocket or in a hip pocket of his trousers. Sneezes, spills, coughs, cuts, wiping, nose blowing and all manner of things can be taken care of easily and tastefully with a handkerchief – not to mention the gentlemanly impression you make when you offer a clean hankie to a woman in need! Much like a Boy Scout, a gentleman with a handkerchief is "always prepared."

A Short Guide to What to Wear When

- *Athletic Event — Casual; at Christ School, School Dress is traditional at football games and other athletic events.*
- *Banquet (Athletic, Fraternity, etc.) — Suit, Jacket, or Blazer with Tie.*
- *Church — Jacket or Blazer with Tie, or a Suit; here one's convictions are far more important than one's costume.*
- *Committee Meeting on Campus — School Dress.*
- *Committee Meeting off Campus — Jacket or Blazer with Tie, or a Suit.*
- *Convocation (Opening) — Jacket or Blazer with Tie.*
- *Dance — Suit or Black Tie.*
- *Debutante Ball — Black or White Tie.*
- *Dinner at an Administrator's or Professor's home — Jacket or Blazer with Tie, or a Suit, unless host or invitation clearly indicates casual dress.*
- *Dinner with a Guest Lecturer or Performer — Jacket or Blazer with Tie, or a Suit.*
- *Evening Lecture on Campus — School Dress.*
- *Evening Lecture off Campus — Jacket or Blazer with Tie, or a Suit.*
- *Funeral — Suit (preferably dark).*
- *Job Interview — Suit or Jacket.*
- *Mixer — School Dress.*
- *Opera — Suit or Black Tie, depending on where you sit and with whom.*
- *Play or Concert off Campus — Jacket or Blazer with Tie, or a Suit.*
- *Reception — Blazer with Tie or a Suit.*
- *Court Trial — Jacket or Blazer with Tie or Suit.*
- *Tour of Campus with Visitor — School Dress is acceptable, although a Jacket or Blazer with Tie is preferable.*
- *Travel when representing Christ School — School Dress, team gear or other, as determined by the coach.*
- *Weddings — Suit or Black Tie.*

CHAPTER 3:

DINING SKILLS

Table Manners
Good table manners should be practiced constantly, at every meal and with any audience. You will find it increasingly difficult to remember to use proper table manners when it is important to do so, if you get accustomed to eating like an orangutan.

Seating
It is polite for children and men to wait for women to take their seats (also to offer assistance with seating) before they sit. A man accompanying a woman to dinner helps to seat her. He should sit opposite her or to the left of her. It is also courteous for the man to offer the woman the most comfortable seat or the seat with the best view.

Eating at a Buffet
Most meals in private homes to which you will be invited, especially when you are young, will be served buffet-style. The majority of young people live in small homes or apartments and do not have domestic help. Your hosts are probably serving as cook, bartender, butler and maid. At a buffet you serve yourself from a table or sideboard, picking up your plate, napkin, fork, occasionally a knife, food and beverage (although this may be served). Find a seat; the wise man finds a chair and table in close proximity. Spread your napkin on your knee or lap and begin eating. Although these dinners require considerable

dexterity, they are informal in feeling (but not necessarily in dress) and conversation is easy. You have only one plate (containing entrée, vegetable, salad and bread), one or two implements, one napkin and one glass to keep up with. When finished, you should carry your plate to the dining room or the kitchen. You will then help yourself to dessert and coffee. Often the plates are collected and dessert and coffee are served.

Posture at the Table
Ideal posture at the table is to sit straight, but not stiffly, leaning slightly against the back of the chair. Your hands, when you are not actually eating, may lie in your lap, which will automatically prevent you from fussing with implements, playing with bread crumbs, drawing on the tablecloth and so forth. However, if you can resist the temptation to fidget, you may rest your hands and wrists – but *not* your entire forearm – on the edge of the table, which may seem more comfortable and less stiff. Hands should also be kept away from the face, from nervous scratching and from twisting or touching the hair.

For all we hear about *"elbows off the table,"* there are some situations when elbows are not only permitted on the table but are actually necessary. This is true in restaurants where to make oneself heard above music or conversation, one must lean far forward. A woman is far more graceful leaning forward supported by her elbows than doubled forward over her hands in her lap as though she were in pain! At *home*, when there is no reason for leaning across the table, there is no reason for elbows. At a formal dinner, elbows may be on the table because again one has to lean forward in order to talk to a companion at a distance across the table. But even in these special situations elbows are *never* on the table *when one is eating.*

Slouching or slumping at the table is most unattractive too. Tipping one's chair – a most unfortunate habit – is unforgivable. It not only looks dreadfully sloppy, but is fatal to the back legs of the chair.

The Blessing
The custom of saying grace or giving thanks for food generally precedes the meal in the United States. Some people choose to stand for the blessing, others remain seated for the blessing, while others may choose

to hold hands while giving thanks. Guests should follow the lead of their hosts. A guest who does not share the same faith is not expected to participate in this religious moment. However, the good guest will show respect by remaining still and silent at this time. In public places, most diners give thanks silently instead of aloud, especially when they are part of a group of diners of mixed religions. A family dining out together may choose to express thanks aloud. However, if you are hosting or leading a group which is dining out, it is best not to impose your religion or practice on others.

Eating at a Formal Dinner

More formal dinners present more challenges. You may take your plate and serve yourself from a sideboard or serving table and then sit down, or the entire meal may be served to you. Plates are served from your left and removed from your right. When passing items around the table, pass to your right. At a seated dinner do not attempt to help with the service unless asked to do so. If asked to pass the salt or pepper, pass both together, not just one.

If you serve yourself, go to the dining table or one of the small tables about the room or house and sit down, after helping the woman next to you with her chair. Usually the ladies serve themselves first and are at the table when you arrive. However, if a woman arrives after you are seated, stand up and help with

A.	Salad Plate	
B.	Salad Fork	G. Water Goblet
C.	Dinner Fork	H. Dessert Spoon and
D.	Dinner Plate and	Fork
	Napkin	I. Bread and Butter
E.	Dinner Knife	Plate with Butter
F.	Soup Spoon	Spreader

her chair. When the entire meal is to be served, you should go to the table and stand behind your chair until all the ladies have been seated. You should assist the woman to your left with her chair. Do not begin eating until everyone has been served. Wait for the hostess to lift her fork or for some other formal opening of the meal to occur, such as a toast or blessing, before you begin. If the group is large, however, it is not necessary to wait until all have been served. The hostess, if she is at all aware of her guests' comfort, will say, as soon as the first two or

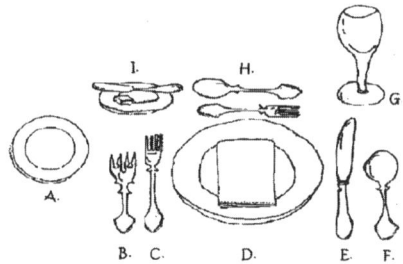

three guests have their food, "Please start – your dinner will get cold if you wait," and the guests take her at her word and start immediately. If the hostess says nothing, and you realize that her attention has been devoted to serving or supervising, or that she has simply forgotten to say anything, it is not incorrect to pick up your spoon or fork after five or six people have been served. The others will soon follow your lead. At family meals, as Mother or Father fills and passes the plates, the children should say, "May I please begin?" if they are not old enough to be expected to wait until one or two adults have started.

Place Settings Explained

When you arrive at the table, a place will have been set. The simplest setting will have only a napkin, a dinner fork to the left of the plate, a dinner knife to the right, a water glass and/or a wine glass at the tip of the knife blade. There may be a bread and butter plate, with a butter spreader, at the tip of the fork tines. The butter spreader will usually be on the butter plate, although it can be set to the right of the knife.

A useful hint to remember when faced with a battery of strange utensils is that, if all is in order in the household where you are a guest, the silverware is set so that it will be used from the outside in toward the plate. Thus, the salad fork is to the left of the dinner fork and the soup spoon is to the right of the knife. When in doubt on how to proceed, follow the host's lead if you can.

Napkin

The napkin is to the left of the dinner fork or in the center of the place setting. Unfold the napkin unobtrusively as soon as you sit down and place it in your lap unless you are at a formal dinner where you should wait for the hostess to put hers on her lap first. A man should never tuck his napkin into his collar, his belt, or between the buttons of his shirt. When using the napkin, avoid wiping your mouth as if with a washcloth. Blotting or patting the lips is much more attractive. If you must leave the table during the meal, place your napkin in your seat (not on the table) while you are away. Your napkin should be laid (not balled up) to the left of your plate when you have finished dinner. However, if a host or hostess is present at the meal, wait for him or her to do this first.

Glasses

If there are multiple glasses at your place, it is good to know what they are for—even if you will not be needing all of them. If there are both a water glass and a wine glass, the wine glass is to the right of the water glass. The water glass will probably be the larger glass. If both white wine and red wine are being served, the white wine glass is in front between the water goblet and the red wine glass. The white wine glass is often smaller than the red wine glass. Glasses for dessert wines are set behind and between the water goblet and the red wine glass. Notice that their degree of accessibility corresponds to the order in which you use them.

Hold long-stemmed water and wine glasses or goblets by the thumb and first two fingers at the base of the bowl of the glass. Hold small stemmed glasses by the stem.

Dining Styles

Four basic dining styles are practiced throughout the world today: American (zigzag) and Continental (European) are the two most prevalent in the United States; Asian and Communal (with the hands) are the others.

American style dining requires that hands remain in the lap except when using silverware. European style dining requires that the hands stay at the table level with the wrists touching the table's edge except when lifting food to the mouth.

Correct American style requires that after a bite of food is cut, the knife be placed at the top of the plate with the blade facing the diner (cut one bite at a time into a reasonable, bite-sized piece). The fork is then transferred to the right hand for eating with the prongs turned upward where it is held with the thumb and index finger about half way up the handle. The middle finger supports the fork while the rest of the fingers gently grasp the handle. The spoon is held in the same fashion. Put down your knife and fork between bites when eating in the American style.

Europeans eat from the fork held in the left hand exactly as when cutting, with the prongs pointed downward. Whereas, this is correct in European countries, it may be misinterpreted as the use of bad manners in some areas of this country. The safest practice here is to follow the saying "When in Rome, do as the Romans do." Therefore, in this country, you should stick to our nation's custom. However, if you are from another country and not familiar with American style dining, it is permissible to stick with that with which you are most comfortable.

When you have finished eating, place the knife and fork in the center of the plate. The knife is above the fork with the blade edge facing inward, from right or left, depending on which hand you use. The handles are just over the rim of the plate. There are two reasons for putting the silver in the center of the plate when you have finished. The first is that there it is less likely to fall off when the plate is removed; the second is that there it tells the server that you have finished. While you are still eating, the silver is laid down temporarily, not across the center, but across the top right quadrant of the plate.

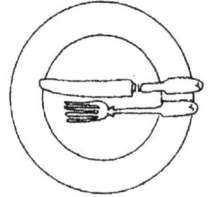

Six Courses of a Meal

1. First Course: Soup, fresh fruit cup, melon or shellfish may be presented during the first course. Sometimes called an appetizer or hors d'oeuvres in the United States.
2. Second Course: Fish or seafood is typically served or sometimes a salad.
3. Third Course: The entrée or main course (usually meat or fowl and vegetables).
4. Fourth Course: Salad. (Salad is often served before the main course in the United States and after the main course in Europe.)
5. Fifth Course: Dessert.
6. Sixth course: Coffee.

Using a Knife and Fork

The dinner fork is held in the right hand, much like you hold a pencil, between thumb and index finger, resting on the middle finger. It should be held at the balancing point so that you can lift

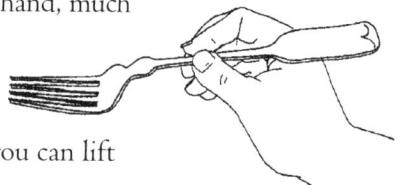

food easily. It should never be filled more than half full, so that it never needs to go more than halfway into your mouth (and so that your bites will not be too big). It should never be clinked against teeth; pull the food off with open teeth and closed lips.

Cutting

When cutting food, hold the fork in your left hand and the knife in your right hand. The fork is held with the tines pointing down. The thumb is below, the index finger above, the handle. The knife is held with the thumb on the inside and the index finger on the top of the handle. In both cases the handle is pressed up into the palm of your hand. Never make a fist around the handle of a fork or knife.

Butter Spreader

The butter spreader may rest on the bread and butter plate or be set to the right of the dinner knife. There is a difference between a butter *spreader*, which is used at each individual place, and a butter *knife*, which is used to cut butter from a common plate and to put butter on your bread and butter plate. Never use your butter spreader to take butter from a common plate or the butter knife to spread butter on your bread. If there is no bread and butter plate or butter spreader (you should not have one without the other), take the butter with the butter knife, put it on your plate and spread it on your bread with your dinner knife.

Often in restaurants and sometime in private homes, you will encounter a butter plate without a butter spreader. Use your dinner knife to spread the butter on your roll and then place it across the top of your butter plate until your dinner plate arrives, at which time you can transfer it to your dinner plate.

Salad Fork

The salad fork will always be with the dinner fork; it is shorter and wider, with a broad tine for cutting. When the salad is served as a separate course before the main course, the salad plate will be in front of you and the salad fork will be to the left of the dinner fork (because you will use it before you use your dinner fork). When the salad is served *with* the main course, the salad fork will be to the right of the dinner fork (because you will start with the main course before the salad) and the salad plate will be to the left of the forks. In either case, when you have finished your salad, leave the fork across the center of the salad plate; both will be removed together. If the salad is served with the main course and there is no salad fork, the salad will be eaten with the dinner fork which is left on the dinner plate when the meal is finished. Never stack your salad plate (or any other dish) on your dinner plate.

Soup Spoon

The soup spoon, which has a rounder bowl than a teaspoon, will be set to the right of the dinner knife. Soup is always served as a separate first course. Spoon the soup *away* from you. Fill the spoon about half or three-quarters full as you push your spoon away from you. Lift the spoon and bring it to your mouth; don't bend down to the bowl. Tilt the spoon toward you and let the liquid flow into your mouth; don't put the spoon all the way into your mouth. This whole process should be accomplished as noiselessly as possible. If necessary, you may tip the bowl away from you. Never leave a soup spoon in the bowl, either between bites or when you have finished. Place it on the plate on which the soup bowl is served.

Teaspoon

The teaspoon is set immediately to the right of the knife, between the knife and the soup spoon. Never leave the spoon in a teacup or coffee cup, as this creates a precarious situation; put it on the saucer as soon as you finish stirring. Do not use your teaspoon to take sugar from the sugar bowl; there should be a sugar spoon.

Dessert Silver

Implements for dessert are properly placed lengthwise above the dinner plate, the bowl of the spoon to the left and the tines of the fork to the right. This is always done in Europe. In the United States, the dessert utensils usually are on the dessert plate. As with soup and teaspoons, dessert spoons should never be left sticking up out of a dish, but should be placed on the saucer under the bowl. If dessert is eaten with a fork, it too should be left on the dessert plate.

Other Silver
There are numerous other eating utensils which you might encounter – cocktail forks, fish knives and forks (seldom in the United States), tongs for escargots and instruments to crack a whole lobster. When in doubt, watch your hosts and do what they do.

Pushers
There is no better pusher than a piece of bread crust. Lacking this, the knife is also correct – if properly used. It is held in the left hand in the same position as when cutting with the right hand and the tip of the blade helps to guide and push the food onto the fork. It is a natural motion and in no way incorrect.

"Please Pass"
It is correct to reach for anything on the table that does not necessitate stretching across your neighbor or leaning far across the table yourself. When something is out of reach, simply ask the person nearest it, "Would you please pass the jelly, Joe?" When an accompaniment that is ordinarily served – butter for the bread, mustard for the ham, salt and pepper, etc.-is not on the table, it is undoubtedly an oversight. You may ask your hostess, "Do you have any mustard, Mrs. Jones?" or "Could we have a little butter for the rolls?" You should not, however, ask for anything unusual, or something that your hostess might not have on hand.

Finger Foods
Some foods are perfect for eating with your hands. Foods that have a "handle" such as shrimp and firm asparagus may also be picked up with your fingers.

Pizza	Artichokes	Olives
Sandwiches without gravy	Grapes	Tortillas
Hamburgers	Corn on the Cob	Hot-Dogs

Sometimes Finger Foods

- *Bacon when it is crisp*
- *Bananas when you are alone, but if it is sliced, eat it with a spoon or fruit fork*
- *French-fries*
- *Fried chicken at picnics*
- *Watermelon when it is not served with utensils — usually outside or at a picnic*
- *Apples when you are alone or on a picnic. Cut and quarter apples in a restaurant*
- *Celery. Eat it by hand. If you like salt, place some on your plate and dip the celery into it.*

EATING OUT

Eating out means consuming a meal outside of your home. We all eat out frequently — most often lunch and too often fast food. Courtesy and good manners always apply, but "dining out" — even if it is at lunchtime — in a fine restaurant is an entirely different experience and can be intimidating until you become comfortable with it.

Dining Out With Restaurant Savvy

Much social entertaining is done in restaurants or the dining rooms of private clubs. There are some conventions unique to restaurants of which you should be aware.

Usually, the first person you encounter is the hostess or maitre d' (hotel), who will have the record of your reservation, if one was made, and will show you to your table. (It is always desirable to make a reservation.) You will be received more graciously and served more efficiently if you make an effort to reserve a table. A restaurant will hold a reservation for fifteen minutes beyond the agreed hour; after that you are on your own. (Telephone if you will be late.) The maitre d' will turn your table over to a server, who may be supervised by a captain and assisted by someone to bus (clear) the dishes; but it is the server with whom you will deal primarily, unless there is some problem which requires the attention of his or her superior.

If you are host and wish to do so, suggest that your guests have a cocktail or aperitif. If you are a guest, especially if it is a business

— related meal, wait for your hosts to suggest before-dinner drinks. If no suggestion is made, do not order one. This is also the procedure for after-dinner drinks.

If you are the host and if you have been to the restaurant before, you may take the initiative and make suggestions to your guests. If you are a guest, ask your host for recommendations. After reading over the menu, you may have questions; do not hesitate to ask your server about a sauce and its ingredients or a method of cooking. However, this question-and-answer period should not be prolonged. When you have selected, close your menu and place it on the table in front of you. When the server sees that all the menus are closed, he or she should return for orders. Women's orders are taken first; women are also served first.

Service

The advice given earlier in this book applies when dining out in a fine restaurant. Assist your date with her chair; the maitre d' or server may do this for you. Some member of the staff may help you with your chair. The table should be set very much as it would be at a formal dinner in a private home, which means you know what all those glasses are used for. Pick up your napkin or remove it from the glass in which it might be displayed and put it on your lap, but don't be surprised if the server picks up your napkin, shakes it out and hands it to you.

You go through the dinner as you would any formal dinner. Contribute to the conversation, enjoy the setting, the food, the drink and the evening.

However, if you are the host and paying the check, you have a responsibility to assure that the service is as it should be. Most fine restaurants take great care to train their staff; but if there is a problem, speak to your server quietly and try to use a question. "Is there a problem in the kitchen?" is preferable to "We have been waiting 45 minutes for our meal." If your server seems to have disappeared, it is perfectly correct to make a simple request (more water, for example) of another server. Excuse yourself from the table, go to the maitre d' station or front desk and state your complaint civilly but in no uncertain terms. Things should never have to get to this point, but it is worth knowing how to handle the matter properly if they do.

If you do not think the food is good, don't take out your displeasure on the server if he or she has performed properly. You may tell the server or maitre d' that you did not like a particular dish, but leave a proper tip.

Food may be sent back to the kitchen if it is overcooked or undercooked contrary to your order, but if you are someone's guest, it is best to eat it as it is rather than upset your hosts.

Settling Up

If you are host, you must settle the bill and the tip. Twenty percent is customary in very good restaurants and fifteen percent in more casual restaurants, although you may certainly leave less if the service has been unsatisfactory, or more if the service has been extraordinary. If you are a guest, don't worry about the bill, although it is always an abuse of hospitality to run up the check by ordering extravagantly. It is always better, if the check is to be divided in some way, to decide this before the meal than to squabble when the check arrives.

MINOR DIFFICULTIES

Food That is Too Hot or Spoiled

If a bite of food is too hot, quickly take a swallow of water. Only if there is no beverage at all, and your mouth is scalding, should you spit it out. And then it should be spit onto your fork or into your fingers and quickly put on the edge of the plate. The same is true of spoiled food. Should you put a "bad" oyster or clam, for example, into your mouth, don't swallow it, but remove it as quickly and unobtrusively as you can. To spit anything whatever into the corner of your napkin is unnecessary and not permissible.

Choking on Meat or Bones

Although we occasionally hear of someone choking to death on a piece of meat, the ordinary "choke" or "swallowing the wrong way" is not serious. If a sip of water does not help, but you think you can dislodge the offending bit by a good cough, cover your mouth with your napkin and do it. Remove the fish bone or abrasive morsel from your mouth with your fingers and put it on the edge of your plate. If you need a more prolonged cough, excuse yourself and leave the table. In the event that you are really choking, don't hesitate to get someone to help you. The seriousness of your condition will quickly be recognized and it is no time to worry about manners. Keeping calm and acting quickly might well save your life.

Coughing, Sneezing and Blowing Your Nose

It is not necessary to leave the table to perform any of these functions, unless the bout turns out to be prolonged. In that case, you should excuse yourself until the seizure has passed. When you feel a sneeze or a cough coming on, cover your mouth and nose with your handkerchief, or if you do not have one, or time to get it out, use your napkin. In an emergency, your hand will do better than nothing at all. Never use your napkin to blow your nose. If you are caught short without a handkerchief or a tissue, excuse yourself and head for the restroom.

Stones, Bugs, Hairs, etc.

When you get something that doesn't belong there in your mouth, there is no remedy but to remove it. This you do as inconspicuously as possible – spitting it quietly into your fingers. But occasionally you notice the foreign matter before you eat it – a hair in the butter, a worm on the lettuce, or a fly in the soup. If it is not too upsetting to you, remove the object without calling attention to it and go on eating. If it is such that is upsets your stomach (as a hair does to many people) leave the dish untouched rather than embarrass your hostess in a private home. At a restaurant you may – and should – point out the error to your waiter and ask for a replacement. Of course an observant host or hostess will spot the problem when he or she notices that you are not eating something and will see that the dish is replaced.

Food Stuck in the Tooth

Toothpicks should not be used in front of others and never at the table. You should certainly not pick at food in your teeth with your finger either. If it is actually hurting, excuse yourself and go to the restroom to remove it. Otherwise wait until the end of the meal and then go to take care of it. *Never* use a toothpick in public or in front of others. Save this task for the privacy of a restroom.

TACKY TABLE OFFENDERS

While it is better to emphasize the positive approach to good manners, there are a number of dining rules that are better expressed by the negative. The most important ones are:

- *Don't cram your mouth with food.*
- *Don't mix food on your plate or food items on your fork.*
- *Don't ever put liquid in your mouth if it is already filled with food unless the food is so hot or spicy that it is burning your mouth. Never blow on food to cool it; wait for it to cool by itself.*
- *Don't encircle a plate with the left arm while eating with the right hand.*
- *Don't push back your plate when finished. It remains exactly where it is until the person serving you removes it. If you wait on yourself, get up and carry it to the kitchen.*
- *Don't lean back and announce, "I'm through," or "I'm stuffed." The fact that you have put your fork or spoon down shows that you have finished.*
- *Don't put your arms or elbows on the table while eating; it is quite correct, however, between courses or after the meal, if the dishes have been removed.*
- *Never reach across the table so far as to necessitate your rising from the seat.*
- *Never shout across the table; speak to everyone near you.*
- *Never smoke during meals. In fact, the best policy is not to smoke at all.*
- *Don't crook your finger when picking up your cup. It's an affected mannerism.*
- *Don't ever leave your spoon in your cup. Not only does it look unattractive; it is almost certain to result in an accident.*
- *Don't leave half of the food on your spoon or fork to be waved about during conversation. One often sees this done with ice cream, but the coldness is no excuse. One should put less on the spoon and eat it in one bite.*
- *Don't cut up your entire meal (or even half of it) before you start to eat; it only makes a mess on your plate.*
- *Don't pile mashed potatoes and peas on top of the meat on your fork — in short, don't take huge mouthfuls of any food.*
- *Don't sop liquid foods up as with bread and gravy.*
- *Don't gesture or point with silverware.*
- *Don't chew food with an open mouth and don't form it into a ball in one cheek. Chew small bites and do not chase your food with a beverage.*
- *Don't talk with food in your mouth.*
- *Don't make noises while eating such as smacking food, making cooing umm. . .*

umm… sounds and crunching ice. Eat and chew as quietly as possible. Try not to repulse others around you.

- *Don't blow your nose, cough or sneeze at the table without covering your mouth. (Excuse yourself from the table for each if you have time. If not, be sure to turn your head away from the table.) Use a handkerchief or tissue, if you have one, and your napkin or hand as a last resort.*
- *Don't scratch or adjust clothing, or comb or arrange your hair at the table.*
- *Don't talk about unappetizing or emotionally charged topics at the table.*
- *Don't leave a mess where someone else must eat.*
- *Don't pick food from your teeth and NEVER use a toothpick in front of others!*

CHAPTER 4:

CORRESPONDENCE

Invitations

All social events begin with an invitation. Invitations to casual social gatherings are often issued over the telephone and usually require an immediate response, but more formal invitations are in writing. It is never incorrect to respond to any written invitation, even if no response is requested. Traditionally, a written invitation requires a reply, but if a telephone number is given on the invitation, then it is acceptable to reply in that manner. *Never fail to respond to an invitation if it is requested that you do so.*

R.s.v.p.

R.s.v.p. is the abbreviation for the French "respond if you please," and you should *always* respond. "R.s.v.p.," "Please reply," or "The favor of a reply is requested" on an invitation means that you *must* say whether you will or will *not* attend. Failure to respond is extremely bad manners and will be noticed by the hosts. "Regrets" or "Regrets only" require a response only if you will not attend. Also, you should respond to an invitation you receive promptly and well in advance of the event (at the very least 48 hours), unless an emergency changes your plans. If you fail to respond but attend anyway, offer some explanation or apology upon arrival. If you fail both to respond and to attend, write or telephone your apologies as soon after the event as possible. If you sent your regrets, do not go unless you contact your host or hostess in advance.

Formal Reply

Sometimes a response card is included with the invitation and simply requires the recipient to fill in a reply and mail back in the envelope provided. If not, a formal invitation should be responded to on a formal, folded note card or letter sheet.

The following form is proper for all formal social functions-dinners, receptions, dances, etc. Remember that with wedding invitations you are responding for the reception, not the ceremony, so word your reply accordingly. You would never use this form for a casual event, when either a simple note or telephone call is quite proper. *More important than the form, however, is the courtesy of a response.* It is not just idle curiosity on the part of your hosts to know whether or not you will attend. They need to know in order to purchase and prepare food, to determine seating arrangements, to employ help, etc.

Mr. Harold Pierre Swanson
regrets that
he is unable to accept
Mr. and Mrs. John Duffy Davenport's
kind invitation to dinner
on Tuesday, the tenth of July

Or

Mr. Steven Huntington Harris
accepts with pleasure
the kind invitation of
Mr. and Mrs. John Duffy Davenport
for Tuesday, the tenth of July
at eight o'clock

E-mail and Answering Machines

It is perfectly correct to respond to an invitation by telephone or by e-mail if the invitation was extended in such a manner. It is also correct, of course, to reply to a written invitation in this manner if the invitation asks you to do so.

When telephoning, it is better to talk to your host on the telephone so try to call when they are likely to be home; but if they are not at home when you call, you may leave a message on an answering machine or voice mail.

While on the subject of answering machines and voice mail, refrain from the immature temptation to have your own off-color or unrefined message or to leave one even as a joke. You never know who will be calling in or who will hit the play button.

SOCIAL EVENTS

At all social functions, large and small, greet your hosts upon arrival. Thank them upon departure. It is not required that you write a note of thanks, except when you are a house guest but it is never improper to do so. In fact, it is always appreciated and it always says something about your upbringing to the person who receives or sees your note of thanks.

Use your common sense at social events. Don't eat and drink excessively even if the food is good. Try to engage everyone in conversation and to be responsive to conversational overtures, but avoid controversial topics which could lead to arguments. There is a difference between a lively and interesting discussion of a topic which welcomes all points of view and the bullying determination of someone to have his or her say regardless of the opinions and sensibilities of others.

Ethnic, religious, racial, sexist, or sexually explicit jokes or stories are more than just a demonstration of insensitivity and bad taste; they can type you as ignorant, prejudiced, or worse. You will hurt yourself and possibly embarrass your fellow guests and hosts. Remember that you were invited because it was thought that your presence would be a positive addition.

What Should I Wear? How Much Should I Eat Before I Go?
As you plan to go to a social event — after you have taken care of the response - you face two questions. What do I wear? What am I going to be fed? Here are some hints to guide you in anticipating what you should wear and how you will be fed.

Breakfast

Occasionally, you will be invited to *social* breakfasts. Take comfort in Oscar Wilde's epigram, "Only dull people are brilliant at breakfast." The time could be from 8:00 to 10:00 a.m. The dress should be casual unless the breakfast precedes some special event – a morning wedding, a baptism, a church service - but this would be indicated on the invitation. Expect to be fed what one normally eats for breakfast. The *business* breakfast increasingly is replacing the business lunch. These require standard business dress – usually a suit and tie.

Brunch

This combination of breakfast and lunch can tend toward one or the other, depending on the time. A brunch may be held as early as 10:00 a.m. or as late as 1:00 p.m. The dress is casual, although a brunch too may precede or follow a formal event, in which case you should dress accordingly. What you are served is largely left to the discretion and imagination of your hosts, but you may expect a full meal. After all, this is technically a substitute for both breakfast and luncheon.

Luncheon

Luncheons seldom begin before noon or after 2:00 p.m. They may be very formal seated events with dozens of guests, elegant table appointments, exotic foods and caterers in attendance, or casual buffets for a few friends. Take your cue from the style of the invitation and the location of the event. An engraved invitation to the Governor's Mansion, the White House or Buckingham Palace, obviously requires a dark suit. A telephone call or note from a friend indicates casual dress, although a tie would not be out of place.

Dinner

Again study the invitation carefully. The more formal the style of invitation, the more prestigious the location, and the later the hour, the more formal the dinner. A dinner may begin as early as 6:00 p.m. or as late as 8:00 p.m. Always assume that a dinner is semiformal unless the invitation clearly indicates "informal" or "casual" dress. If the dinner, or any social event, is formal, the invitation will specify "Black Tie" or "White Tie."

Supper

Suppers are intimate meals which usually follow a dance, a concert, the theatre or the opera. You wear what is appropriate for the preceding event, if there is one. The meal is usually light. The time is from about 10:00 p.m. to 1:00 a.m. Around 1:00 a.m. the meal is usually called a breakfast and you are back to bacon and eggs.

Other Social Events

Standard meals are relatively easy to handle, but now we must move into the grey areas of receptions, at homes, open houses, teas, desserts and cocktail parties.

Receptions

A reception is usually semiformal or formal. It may stand alone, or precede or follow just about anything, and be in honor of just about anyone. It is usually held in the late afternoon or early evening. The time is usually flexible and the invitation reads something like "four to six o'clock." This means you may come at any time during this period. Never arrive before the first hour stated. Social convention requires that you stay at least one hour. Be sure to stay no more than one hour beyond the last hour stated on the invitation.

Weddings

Wedding receptions may be traditional receptions or, in actuality, luncheons or dinners or dances or cocktail parties. Always wear a dark suit, white shirt and a plain tie to afternoon and evening weddings. If it is a formal wedding (after 6:00 p.m.) where the groom and attendants wear formal dress, the male guests usually wear dinner jackets. A blazer with solid trousers or a light-colored suit (especially in the summer) is proper for a morning wedding, even if it is formal (groom and attendants in cutaways or strollers).

At Homes, Open Houses

An "At Home" or "Open House" is less formal than a reception, although very casual dress is not usually acceptable; coat and tie are recommended. Again the hour is often flexible, the food and drink are often simple. The mood is lighter and the guests fewer if for no other reason than the receptions are usually held in large public rooms while an "At Home" is just that – a party at home. You should stay for at least an hour.

Teas
Teas are the ancestors of cocktail parties although usually a great deal more refined. Food and refreshments are light. The hour is around 4:00 p.m. They may be informal with a few guests or very formal and very large. Dress accordingly; again the tone of the invitation should be your guide.

Cocktail Parties
Cocktail parties are relatively modern inventions. They usually begin around 5:00 p.m. and can go on forever, although they should end by about 8:00 p.m. They may involve a few friends seated comfortably in the living room or a thousand people packed into a drafty ballroom, clawing their way to the bar and buffet table, desperately trying to hear and to be heard. Some cocktail parties are quite pleasant – the crowd well proportioned to the space, the food plentiful and good, and the conversation interesting. If the invitation reads "Cocktail Buffet," ample food is implied although not guaranteed. You should stay at least one hour and dress in accordance with the tone of the invitation.

Desserts
A dessert usually begins after 7:00 p.m. but can be much later. You are invited for sweets, coffee and perhaps after dinner refreshments. Dress in a jacket or blazer with tie, or a suit. Stay an hour at least.

Leaving the Event
Upon leaving the party or event, always thank the hosts and give a sincere compliment about the evening. Examples are how much the ceremony or party has been enjoyed, how beautiful the flowers/ decorations are, how lovely/handsome the host/hostess looks, how delicious the food was.

Always thank your hosts and say goodbye before you get your coat. Avoid saying goodbye to your host with your coat over your arm as this is just as bad manners as saying goodbye to your host after you've put on your coat.

THANK YOU NOTES

People who do nice things for you appreciate knowing that you like what they have done for you. Saying "thank you" is one way to let them know that you are grateful. In our modern times of electronic communication, emails and faxes are additional ways to send an instant message of appreciation. However, the personal touch of a handwritten note has yet to be replaced. The famous Crane ad is true, "To our knowledge no one has ever cherished a fax."

Writing a thank you note does not need to take a lot of time, but its impact can be great. The sooner you write the note, the less you'll need to write. *The important thing to do is to write it.* People will appreciate your written thanks whether you write the note in pencil on notebook paper or on fine vellum. Remember, *good manners refer to the treatment of people the way they wish to be treated while etiquette refers to the written social rules which have evolved in a particular culture.* American etiquette dictates the preferred color of ink as black for a note and that special selections of paper be used for different types of correspondence.

General Good Manners for Writing a Thank You Note
Thank people for having you as a guest for a special meal, party, overnight visit, gift or for anything they have done especially nice for you such as help you with a difficult project.

- *Write and send your written note within a week after someone has done something special for you.*
- *Write your note on clean, nice paper.*
- *Use your best penmanship. Be neat.*
- *Use good grammar and look up the correct spelling of any words you do not know how to spell.*
- *Write your note as though you were talking to the person.*
- *Specify the kindness and tell why you appreciate it.*
- *Include a personal note about you and your family.*
- *Add something personal, fun, or nice.*
- *Try to avoid beginning your thank-you note with "Thank you for…..." For example, begin the note by saying something like "It was so much fun to be at your house Friday night," or "I appreciate you remembering me on my graduation."*

Example of a Note to Someone Who Helped You

Dear Mrs. Teeter,

I really appreciate your help in preparing me for the International Student Exchange program in Spain. I just got a letter saying that I have been accepted for a placement in Madrid. I can hardly wait! The time you spent with me helped me to prepare for the conversational part of my interview which went very well. Thanks so much for making yourself available when I needed you.

Sincerely,
Matt

Example of a Note to Someone Who Had You as a Weekend Houseguest

Dear Ms. Davenport,

I had a great time in Wilmington and appreciate you having me for the weekend. It was great to get a chance to surf since I don't get to the beach often. We also had a blast tubing behind the boat. It was all so much fun.

I hope that Simms will come home with me some time later this year when we can go skiing and snowboarding.

Thanks again for your hospitality. I hope I have a chance to come back soon.

Sincerely,
Billy

Example of a Well Written Thank You Note

Dear Aunt Carol,

The paint ball equipment is awesome. The mask, hopper, elbow, co2 tank and round of paint are just what I wanted. My friends and I are going out in the woods this weekend where we won't make a mess when we play paintball. I can't wait.

How do you, Uncle Pat and my cousins Ginny, Katie and John like living in Japan? I bet it is interesting learning about the Japanese customs and traditions. We are thrilled that Uncle Pat was assigned there. He'll provide excellent leadership as Captain.

Our family is fine. Hanna is dancing almost every day. Dad stays busy at the hospital and Mom still finds new flowers to plant and weeds to pull in the garden.

We hope to see you and the rest of the family during Thanksgiving.

Thanks again for a great present.

Love,
Chris

Stationery to Use for Writing a Thank You Note

The hand written note is a powerful tool in today's technological world. Receiving a hand addressed letter on high quality stationery is much more gratifying than a curled, faded, word processed note that arrived via facsimile. Have a supply of note cards or correspondence cards in your desk – it takes only a few minutes to write a quick note.

Everyone should have a box of plain, personalized letter sheets. These are the appropriate papers for replying to formal invitations or writing condolence letters.

A vast array of social stationery is available today ranging from formal to casual in style. Following is a list of some of the types of stationery you may want to have as you correspond with family and friends,

Correspondence Cards for Men (and Women)

Correspondence cards are heavy weight cards marked with your name or monogram. They are available in plain ecru or white, as well as bordered, and in a variety of colors. They range in style from very formal to casual and are used for brief notes, thank you notes, holiday greetings and birthday wishes. Writing should be on the front side only. Place the correspondence card into its envelope bottom edge first with the writing facing the envelope flap so it will be most easily seen when the card is removed from its envelope. Men sometimes use correspondence cards instead of notes.

Half Sheets for Men (and Women)
The half sheet is stationery paper that folds in half to fit in its envelope. Half sheets may be printed or engraved with a monogram, name and/or address. They are used for letters and thank you notes. Avoid writing on the back of the sheet for a longer message. If you need room for a longer message, use a plain second sheet.

Men's Formal Social Writing Paper
Men use single sheets of good heavy quality paper that fits into a rectangular envelope when the sheet is folded once across the center. Black ink is used and writing does not continue onto the back of the sheet.

Calling Cards
Calling cards are believed to have originated in China when communication was conducted in one of two ways – by letter or face to face conversation. The custom of making social calls to the homes of friends was therefore very important. The calling card was designed for use by the visitor to leave behind at the residence of the person who was not at home at the time of the call. A modern use for calling cards is as an enclosure or gift card and they are used both by children and adults.

Envelopes
The return address is correctly placed on the center of the back flap of an envelope containing a social note. The U.S. Postal Service, however, prefers the return address be placed on the front of the envelope on the upper left-hand corner, but does not require it.

Start the address in the middle of the envelope. Write the name of the person the letter is to on the first line. Be sure to include the person's correct title. On the second line, write the street address; and on the third line, write the city, state (which should be spelled out) and zip code. The city and state are separated with a comma.

Post Cards
Post cards are used for brief and informal communications. It is preferable to write all formal correspondence (including thank you notes) on correspondence cards, half sheets or formal stationery.

However, it is also acceptable to use a post card for an informal response and for thank you notes when there is enough space on the card to produce a proper and thorough note.

Note: Christ School students should remember to always send a thank you note after returning to school from an overnight visit to a friend's home.(An exception to this rule is when it is a home that you visit frequently, in which case a thank you is not required after every visit.) Christ School stationery and/or post cards will be available for these purposes in the office of Student Life. Office personnel will gladly assist you with locating proper names and addresses, stamping your correspondence and expediting your courteous thank you. Merits will also be given to those students completing a well written thank you note.

CHAPTER 5:

PERSONAL SKILLS THAT MAKE A DIFFERENCE

The cardinal principal of etiquette is thoughtfulness. This implies a concern for the effect of your actions on those round you. Attracting attention to oneself, because it is usually objectionable to others, is contrary to that basic principle. Just by keeping this one thought in mind, you can save yourself and others embarrassment in many situations.

Good Grooming
You demonstrate respect for yourself and others by the way you present yourself. Good grooming shows that you care about your appearance and that you are concerned about making a good impression. It also shows that you care about the comfort of others.
- Good grooming begins with taking care of your body and its general physical condition. The problem of obesity in this country presents a challenge for those who care about their appearance and want to make a good impression on others.
- Grooming basics begin with a daily bath or shower.
- Rinse all soap from your body and all shampoo from your hair.
- Use a nailbrush on finger nails, elbows, toes and heels.
- Wash your hair when needed. Some people need to shampoo their hair every day; those with very dry hair may be able to wash their hair only a few times a week.
- Don't forget to wear deodorant. In the United States, body odor is

offensive to others and is an indication of poor personal hygiene and grooming.

Dental Details
- Brush and floss your teeth properly at least twice a day.
- Ask your dentist to demonstrate correct brushing if you feel you aren't brushing properly.
- Brush your teeth before bed.
- If the bristles of your toothbrush are worn out or splayed, you are brushing too roughly and it is time for a new brush.
- Brush in a gentle circular motion – gum damage can occur if you scrub too hard.
- Lightly brush your tongue.

Note: Halitosis can be caused by poor dental hygiene as well as other things. Severe cases can not only turn away some of your closest friends and business associates but, most likely, any female you might wish to keep in close company! Be Smart. Brush and floss your teeth daily. If you do so and still have this problem, discuss it with your dentist or your physician.

Fingernails
Both men and women need to take care of their fingernails. Your nail supplies should include, at a minimum, a nail file or emery board and nail clippers. Keep your fingernails clean and trimmed regularly and your toenails clipped. These are small details but people take notice.

Personal Habits
Acceptable personal habits vary from nation to nation. Behavior that is polite in one country may be considered rude in others. For example, burping after a meal is a sign of satisfaction and is encouraged after a meal in some areas. In the United States it is considered terribly impolite to burp in public. Learn the customs and traditions of the people you visit. In the United States of America, do as polite Americans do:
- *AVOID burping and other gaseous expulsions*
- *AVOID cleaning your ears in public*
- *AVOID picking your nose in public*
- *AVOID picking your teeth in public*

- *AVOID talking about the cost of your or others' belongings*
- *AVOID telling secrets in front of others*
- *AVOID scratching in public*
- *AVOID smacking and popping gum*
- *AVOID spitting – unless it is absolutely necessary (hocking and spitting out a wad of phlegm is **NOT** necessary-neither is spitting out of a car window)*
- *AVOID swearing and using profanity*
- *ALWAYS cover your mouth when coughing or sneezing*
- *ALWAYS use a handkerchief or tissue when you blow your nose*
- *ALWAYS excuse yourself from the table when experiencing a coughing or sneezing attack*
- *ALWAYS flush the toilet*
- *Men ALWAYS raise and lower the toilet seat when and after using the toilet*

Bathroom Etiquette

- If you use the last of the shampoo, toothpaste, or toilet paper, let the family grocery shopper know. If you use the last of the toilet paper, put another roll on the dispenser.
- Wipe the drops of water from around the sink after you wash your hands.
- Rinse the bowl of the sink after you brush your teeth.
- Flush the toilet and close the toilet lid after you use it.
- Wipe the hair off the floor after you brush your hair. Clean the hair from the drain after you shower or bathe.
- Fold your towel neatly and hang it up after you use it. Do not refold a guest towel so that someone else will mistake it for unused. Avoid using the host's personal towels unless no guest towels have been left out for you and you have no other towels to use.
- Attendants in public bathrooms should be tipped fifty cents or more if they provide some special services.

Kitchen Etiquette

- Always wash you hands with soap before cooking, eating or making yourself a drink or snack.
- Don't leave your dishes on the table, the counter or in the sink. Rinse them and put them in the dishwasher. Put detergent in and start the dishwasher when it is full. If it is filled with clean dishes, empty the

dishwasher and then load your dirty dishes.

- Wipe the counter and around the sink when you are finished. Pick up the ice cubes you drop on the floor. If you spill something in the refrigerator, wipe up the mess.
- Tell the grocery shopper in your home, or the home you are visiting, when you use the last of something or write it on a list. In addition, if you finish a box or carton of something, throw the empty container or wrapping away.
- If you see something unusual or interesting in the refrigerator, ask before you begin snacking. Those may be ingredients for something special.
- Refill the ice cube trays after taking a few cubes. Don't just put the empty trays back in the freezer.

Magic Words

At some time your mother told you that there is a magic word which will help you get what you want. The word is "please" – and your mother was right. "Please" and "Thank you" have fallen into such disuse that fast food chains have found they must teach their employees to use them as part of customer relations training.

The words we choose to use can help us get what we want and help people have a good feeling when they are around us. Use the following words often and you will see doors open to you as if by magic!

Thank you	*I'm sorry*	*After you*
You first	*Please*	*Your choice*
You choose	*Great job*	*May I?*
Good going	*I need your help*	*Great idea*
Excuse me	*Congratulations*	*Pardon me*
Good thinking	*You're great, smart, fun*	

Words to Avoid

Do not let profanity become a natural part of your vocabulary, or you will find it difficult to avoid using it at inappropriate times. We all get mad; we all swear at ourselves or our frustration or the stupidity of our own actions. We use the words because we know them and we are too upset to think of any more elegant expressions of how we feel. This is not desirable, but it is human and very difficult from peppering your everyday speech with expletives or using profanity to express surprise or emotion. Such speech does not make you sound tough or clever, only vulgar.

Sportsmanship

Most of us will participate in sports activities throughout our lives. Not only do sports provide physical exercise, they teach us to work together as a team and help us develop self-confidence. They also provide a social outlet for both children and adults. Sports etiquette is not always spelled in the rules, but it should be understood and practiced if a player wants to be known as sportsmanlike.

We've all witnessed unbecoming behaviors during sporting events. Not everyone can be the best or be the winner all the time. But you'll enjoy yourself and will be a valuable asset to your team if you remember the points listed below.

- *Remember, there is no "I" in TEAM. Do your part by learning the rules of every game you play so you can play fair.*
- *Never give up. (Persistence is a sign of strength and character.)*
- *Practice self-discipline. Control your temper. Assume responsibility and don't blame others.*
- *Be loyal to your team. Encourage teammates always.*
- *Lead by example.*
- *Respect your opponents. Remember they work as hard as you do to succeed. Good sports do not do anything to distract people from playing the game.*
- *Be a gracious winner and a gracious loser. Both are short-lived. Good sports do not complain about the rules, the coach or the referee. Good losers do not make excuses for their performance or the performance of their teammates. Compliment the winner on his performance after a game. When you are the winner, console the loser on his loss, but not on his performance.*
- *Welcome challenges with enthusiasm.*
- *Welcome constructive criticism. Be able to take it as well as you give it.*
- *Be willing to give more than you take.*
- *See opportunity in every difficulty.*
- *Smile — a gentle curve which straightens many things.*
- *Be committed to your goals. Visualize them always.*

• *Take care of your body. Practice good nutrition, exercise regularly and maintain a healthy weight so you'll feel up to the challenge. Do not abuse your body. Tobacco and drugs are some typical ways to abuse your body. Tattoos, piercings and other fads of the day which add shock value to your appearance may also be viewed as a means of abusing your body. You should treat your body as the vessel that will carry you through life. This means respecting it, caring for it, preserving it, and not defacing or abusing it. Take care of it. It's the only body you have and with any luck it will last you for a long time.*

How to Deal with Prejudice

Unfortunately, we still hear the voice of prejudice from time to time in our society. Ethnic or tasteless jokes, name-calling, sweeping generalizations. What do you do upon finding yourself in such a situation?

If alone, you should feel no need to laugh or silently support such a display of poor taste. Depending on the situation, and the audience, you may choose to comment on the tasteless remark by saying something like this:

• "That's not funny."
• "I don't appreciate your remark/joke and don't think it's funny."
• "I find that comment extremely offensive. Most educated people in today's society have outgrown that mode of thinking/joke telling."
• "I can't believe what you just said."

Or, if you prefer, you may simply get up and leave the room.

If, however, you have with you friends of a minority group about whom the jokes and slurs are being made, your situation is embarrassing. Try to change the conversation if you can. If you cannot, avoid the urge to rise to the defense; it might evoke an onslaught even more embarrassing to your friends. Keep your silence. Break away as soon as possible and apologize to them profusely in private.

If you yourself belong to a minority group under attack, you have two courses. One, you can ignore it, registering in your mind that these are people to be avoided in the future. Or two, you can teach them a lesson that may temper their prejudice in the future. Just say, "You must be talking about me." I'm a (whatever it is)." Their shocked embarrassment will be almost as rewarding as their limp efforts to make amends.

APPEARING IN PUBLIC

Walking on the Street

Years ago it was considered necessary for a man walking with a woman to stay between her and the street to protect her from runaway or obstreperous horses. The most dangerous thing he might protect her from today would likely be the splash of a passing automobile going through a mud puddle.

While the old rule is no longer a necessity, most women feel more feminine and "cared for" when their escorts follow the established pattern. A man need not hop back and forth each time they cross the street, but when they are continuing in the same relative position for some time, he should walk on the outside. Otherwise, if he prefers to ignore the curbside rule entirely, he should always walk on the woman's left.

A man should not sandwich himself between two women when walking or sitting with them. From one side he can look in the direction of both while talking with either one; whereas when he is between them he must turn away from one when he talks to the other. In addition if the women happen to be intimate friends, they may have a tendency to talk "across" him forcing him to turn back and forth as if he were at a tennis match.

Today, a man rarely offers his arm to a woman in the daytime unless she is old and infirm. At night, if a woman is going down steps or a slope while wearing high heels, she is wise to accept his arm, not only because it is a courtesy but it can be difficult to manage when it is too dark to see clearly where one is walking.

A man also offers his arm to a woman when he takes her into a formal dinner or when he is an usher at a wedding. Otherwise couples walk side by side rather than hand on arm.

A man does not grab a woman by the arm or the elbow and shove her along. It is only when he is helping her into a car, a taxi or a bus, or up steep stairs that he should put his hand under her elbow. A man may also take a woman's hand and precede her through a crowd to make way for her.

Ladies — or Gentlemen — First

In most circumstances, indoors or out, when a couple walks together, the woman precedes the man. But over rough ground he goes first and offers his hand if she needs assistance. He steps ahead of her to open a car door for her when he enters it, and he gets out first and holds the door for her when they arrive, unless she doesn't want to wait.

He precedes her down a steep or slippery stairway. However, he follows her up or down an escalator, unless she asks him to go first to help her on or off. Although the idea of protecting her is quite out of key with, and in some cases repugnant to, the capable woman of today, he should make the gesture of stepping into a boat first or off the bus first, for example; to be ready to help her, but should tell her why he is doing so ("Let me step ahead and I will give you a hand").

Femininity is still more attractive in a woman than masculine capability and in no way denies the fact that her helplessness is a thing of the past.

Going Through Doors

A man should always stand aside and allow a woman to pass through an open door ahead of him. When approaching a closed, heavy door, however, it is far more practical and simpler if he pushes the door open, goes through and holds the door while she follows. If the door opens toward them he pulls it open and allows her to go through first.

A woman steps into a revolving door ahead of a man if it is already moving or if there is a partition in such a position that he can push it to start the door turning. Otherwise he steps in first and gets the door moving slowly so that she may step into the section behind him.

Any courteous person — man or woman — holds a door open for the person following him, unless that person is some distance behind. It is extremely rude (but unfortunately very common) to let a door slam shut in someone's face.

Ladies on the Right

Years ago there was a rule of great importance. A lady was never seated on a gentleman's left, because according to the etiquette of the day, a woman "on the left" was not a "lady." But today in America all that remains of this rule is that, when equally practical, it is always more polite that a gentleman seat a lady on his right. (The few surviving rules about placing a lady on the gentleman's right include: the seating of a guest of honor on the right of the host , hostess or chairman and the bride walking down the aisle on her father's right and sitting on the bridegroom's right at all wedding festivities.)

Displaying Affection in Public
Kissing and various forms of petting, fondling and amorous caresses are personal matters and should take place in private. Public displays of physical attraction are often embarrassing to the observer. Ardent embraces, passionate kisses, etc. (in spite of the current race to portray sex in all forms in movies, theaters, TV and literature) can only be as meaningful as they should be when they do not become public property.

This, however, has little to do with the casual, affectionate kiss or hug with which we greet an old friend, or with a couple strolling companionably hand in hand. Men and women who are not more than good friends frequently greet each other with a brief kiss – not on the lips – and it is in no way offensive.

The best way to foil a friend who is a compulsive kisser is to hold out your hand quickly when you meet and use the handclasp to hold her (or him) off. She or he may try anyway, but hold your ground, because if you are overpowered, there is no remedy but to turn a "cold cheek."

Public Transportation
Courtesy is important for the enjoyment and safety of all passengers using public transportation. Obvious common courtesies apply here as they do elsewhere:
- Wait your turn to board. Do not push or break in line.
- Say "Hello" and "Good-bye" to the driver.
- Take your seat and remain seated. It is dangerous to walk around when a bus, train or subway is moving.
- Avoid yelling or screaming as it is distracting to all and could easily cause an accident.
- Keep your possessions with you and out of the way of other passengers at all times.
- Do not leave trash, discarded papers, gum or empty containers on the vehicle. Do your part to leave your seat clean for the next person - even if it means throwing away trash.

Today, with women demanding equal rights in every field, men cannot be expected to treat them as the delicate petals they were supposed to be many years ago. A man who has worked all day is just as tired as the woman next to him on the bus. If he has been fortunate enough to find a seat and the woman standing in front of him does not appear to be elderly, infirm, pregnant or burdened with a baby or a heavy armful of any sort, he need not offer her his place. Of course he may do so if he wishes and she may accept his offer, or not, as she wishes.

Young people, however, should be taught to offer their seats to older people, both men and women. Youngsters are strong, they have not generally worked as hard, and furthermore, it is a gesture of courtesy and respect. A youngster traveling with his or her mother or father should offer the parent the empty seat and it is up to the latter to accept if he or she wants to, or perhaps they may take turns.

Public Cleanliness

The subject is not a pleasant one, but no one can be unaware of the increasing messiness (at times actual filthiness) of the lounges and rooms of hotels, theaters and other public places.

In writing this, there are certain persons to whom this is specifically targeted. At one extreme there are those who are really untidy. We all know people who throw trash no matter where, set messy or dirty items down on no matter what, drop wet raincoats on the nearest upholstered chair and burn table edges with forgotten cigarettes. People leave hairs in the sink and sometimes blow their nose into the air instead of a tissue (yuck!).

In the second group are those who are careless because they take it for granted that someone will come along after them with a dust pan and broom. These people, if made to realize there is no one other than themselves to tidy up, would ordinarily be more careful.

If only all of us who care about our surroundings would be become sufficiently conscious of our obligation to act as deputy wardens, the situation would be improved. In short, instead of refraining from showing criticism of others, it is sometimes our obligation to do what we have been trained not to do – frankly, to correct them. For example, when a person tosses a used paper towel at a receptacle and leaves it lying on the floor when it misses its mark, one should suggest he/she make more effort by picking it up yourself, saying, "Did you notice that you missed the basket?" It would help, perhaps, if the signs seen in many restrooms saying *"Please leave this restroom as you found it,"* read instead *"Please leave this restroom cleaner than you found it."* But signs seem to do little good. Having an attendant on duty seems to be the greatest help – people apparently take a little more care if they feel they are being watched. This is a sad commentary, but in the case of restrooms – true!

Perhaps the most flagrant examples of sheer thoughtlessness are the people who carelessly throw all manner of trash into toilets. In restrooms that have no attendants, conditions are sometimes so bad that there is no answer other than a locked door. The owner of a department store was forced to hang a large sign on the door to the customers' restroom that read *"This restroom can remain open for your convenience only for so long as you cooperate in helping to keep it in order."*

Every city has the same problem in keeping its streets clean. All the campaigns, the special "Keep Our City Clean" weeks, the signs, the trash cans on corners and the fines imposed for littering fail to solve the problem completely. As in the public restroom it is the duty of each and every one of us to take pride in keeping our cities and towns places clean and beautiful and to impress upon others the importance of the problem.

Umbrellas

When a man and woman are walking together, he generally holds the umbrella, if they have only one, since he is presumably taller. If there is a great difference in their heights the woman should carry an umbrella of her own, because one held far above her head will not keep her dry. Both men and women should be very careful not to poke other pedestrians with the umbrella point. Never walk with an umbrella held so that you cannot see ahead. Plastic umbrellas and bubbles are excellent for this reason. When the umbrella is closed it should be held over the arm by the crook or strap so that it hangs close to one's side, rather than crosswise or with the point protruding in any way.

Chewing Gum

It is hard to understand why so many otherwise attractive people totally destroy their appearance by chewing gum like a cow chewing a cud.

There are people who chew it for therapeutic reasons as well as because they like the taste and others just chew because it's a habit. Chewing gum, in itself, if it is done quietly and unobtrusively, is not unattractive. But when one does it with grimaces, open mouth, smacks, crackles and pops, and worst of all with bubbles, it is annoying to people around and is in the worst of taste.

It should be unnecessary to remind people not to dispose of gum where anyone can possibly sit on it, step on it or touch it. But is there anyone who has not been a victim of this thoughtlessness? When you are through with your gum, wrap it in any scrap of paper and throw it in a trash can. If no trash basket is available, keep the gum, wrapped, in your pocket until you find an appropriate place to dispose of it.

Mints also taste good, refresh the breath and don't require the sight and sound effects of gum. It is wise to keep mints handy (if you like them) for times when gum smacking and the movement of mouth and jaw would be noticeably bothersome to others.

Follow these simple chewing gum rules:
- *Never let chewing gum be seen or heard.*
- *Remove your chewing gum when talking on the phone as chewing sounds are transmitted to others.*
- *Dispose of chewed gum permanently. The street, sidewalk, behind the ear or under the table or dinner plate is not acceptable.*
- *Never take a stick of gum for yourself and not offer one to others. Offer half of a stick of gum if you have only one or wait until you are alone if several people are present.*

Places to avoid chewing include:
- *Classrooms where listening and concentration are necessary,*
- *Places of worship that are deemed holy,*
- *Theatres and musical events where people are listening, and*
- *Museums and libraries where silence is requested and valuable objects may be ruined by gum that might unexpectedly pop out of the mouth.*

Helpful Hint: Peanut butter will remove ABC (already been chewed) gum from hair and skin.

Smoking

Smoking started in an era when there was not yet evidence available to prove the likelihood of it compromising a person's health or causing their death. Today, the evidence clearly shows both to be true and confirms the serious health risks a person takes when they decide to smoke (or to use tobacco products in other ways). Though it doesn't take a rocket scientist to know whether or not it is a good idea to use tobacco, there are still some people who choose to do so.

If you choose to smoke – despite the health warnings and risks – you should be aware of how highly offensive this practice may be to others. Because of this and the health risks to others from second hand smoke, smoking regulations are becoming more prevalent in all places from public restaurants and building to private homes. The best rule of thumb in today's world is to not smoke unless a function is outside or it is clear that smoking is acceptable. Always ask those around you if they mind if you smoke. If they do, go somewhere else where you will not bother others while you smoke.

As evidenced by the warning printed on their containers, "Smokeless tobacco is **not** a safe alternative to cigarettes." If, however, you choose to ignore this warning and use these products, you should know that this product is the leading cause of oral cancer and its use can also be as offensive to others as tobacco smoke. Use of any of these products is viewed as being in very poor taste by many people.

Alcohol

Whether or not one drinks alcoholic beverages is a matter of personal choice. Where, when and how one drinks, however, are social and legal concerns.

The legal drinking age is 21. To disregard this or any other law – such as those concerning illegal drugs – can have serious consequences.

Those who are of the age to drink should also know that in many states, including North Carolina, drinking in public (without a permit, such as at a public affair) is illegal.

If you choose to drink alcohol, you will learn early in your experience to find your low risk limit; learn to respect that limit. A number of factors affect the amount a person can consume before becoming impaired or drunk – no longer in rational control of his actions.

Do not fool yourself. Unless you are a person with alcoholism, you *do* know when you are impaired and you *can* stop drinking. Excessive, high risk consumption of alcohol is insulting to your hosts and companions; it never enhances your desirability as a guest, a date or a participant in any civilized activity and usually leads to problems – personal, social and academic.

If you set out to get drunk, you will, and when you are drunk, it is never as much "fun" as you thought it would be when you were sober. If you set out repeatedly to get drunk, this is quite possibly a sign of a serious emotional or physical problem. Please seek help.

There is a huge difference between social drinking and drunkenness. Drunkenness can make your behavior irrational, offensive or violent. It can lead to health problems, addiction, unsafe sex, date rape or jail. Drunkenness prevents the brain from performing fully; the ability to think analytically can be impaired for as long as a week. Driving while impaired is dangerous and illegal; driving while drunk is suicidal or homicidal. Acute alcohol intoxication can kill you.

You are always legally and morally responsible for your actions, drunk or not. What one chooses to do to himself is ultimately that person's responsibility; however, when your actions have negative consequences for others, the line is crossed, and your actions become the business of others, especially those who must put up with your behavior or clean up the mess – literally and figuratively.

Behind the Wheel

Good manners are not suspended when you get behind the wheel of an automobile. A good driver is knowledgeable, alert, cautious and sober. A courteous driver is one who is sensitive to the needs and predicaments of other drivers and who does not react negatively to the aggressive rudeness of others. A good and courteous driver is always alert to and respectful of pedestrians, runners, bicyclists, and others who share the roads with motorists. A courteous driver avoids using the horn, keeps the volume of the stereo at a reasonable level and ignores the rude behavior of others.

Good Posture

There is no doubt that a person – man or woman- who stands and sits erect looks best. A round-shouldered slouch, with head thrust forward and stomach sticking out, certainly does little to make one appealing. Victorian parents used to insist that children sit up straight and even the youngsters who hated that admonition grew to appreciate it. Today it is common to see young people sprawling, slouching and in all manner of contortions, with no one saying a word about it. But it is worth fussing about and children will eventually thank their parents for encouraging them to "Stand up straight!"

Men often have less problem sitting properly than women, because wearing trousers allows more latitude. As long as they do not slump way down in their seats wrap their legs into pretzels or thump or jerk nervously, they may sit pretty much as they please, with both feet on the floor, or one leg crossed over the other above the knee.

Good posture not only looks better and makes a person more attractive but it also helps prevent other health problems that may develop as a person ages.

CHAPTER 6:

SOCIAL SKILLS THAT MAKE A DIFFERENCE

CONVERSATION SKILLS

If you dread meeting strangers because you are afraid you won't be able to think of anything to say, remember that most conversational errors are committed not by those who talk too little but by those who talk too much.

Many people, for some reason, are terrified of silence and they generally have great difficulty carrying on a conversation. This terror is something like the terror felt by those who are learning to swim. It is not just the first stroke that overwhelms them, but the thought of all the strokes that must follow. The frightened talker doesn't hear a word that is said by others because he or she is trying so desperately to think of what to say next. So the practical rule for continuing a conversation is the same as that for swimming. Don't panic. Just take it one stroke (or word) at a time.

Fishing for Topics

In talking to a person you have just met and about whom you know nothing, the best approach is to try one topic after another just as a fisherman searches for the right fly. You try for nibbles by asking a few questions. When one subject runs down, you try another. Or perhaps you take your turn and describe something you have been doing or thinking about – planning a trip, starting a band or an interesting article you have read. Conversation is not a race that must be continued at breakneck pace to the finish line.

When you find yourself seated next to a stranger at a party, introduce yourself before starting your "fishing." Then there are all kinds of openings, and if you are shy, have some of them fixed in your mind before you go to the party. If your hostess has told you something about your dinner partner, you might say, "I understand you crewed for James in the race last week. That must have been exciting." If you know nothing about him at all, you could ask, "Do you live in Asheville or are you visiting?" From his answer, hopefully, you can carry on a conversation. He will probably ask where you live and what you do. It's simple enough, but be sure to give him the opportunity to talk.

Another helpful tidbit — and one that wins instant popularity- is to ask advice. "We are planning to drive through the South. Do you know any particularly good places to stop on the way?" or "I'm thinking of buying a new laptop computer. Do you have any suggestions?" In fact, it is safe to ask his or her opinion on almost anything: sports, the stock market, a current fad — anything.

The food or the meal provides another good opener at the dinner table: "Isn't this delicious — what do you think Joe's mom put into this sauce to make is so unusual?"

And don't always avoid a controversial subject when trying to make conversation. In an election year "Who do you support," or "What do you think of the vice-presidential candidates?" will start the ball rolling with no effort at all.

Humor: The Rarest Gift of All

There are those who can tell a group of people that their train broke down or that they had a flat tire and make everyone burst into laughter. But the storyteller who constantly *tries* to be funny is generally a bore and the majority of us, if we wish to be considered attractive, are safer if we rely on sincerity, clarity and an intelligent choice of subject.

If your friend Alan is both interesting and amusing, you will, if you are wise, do everything you can to lure him to your house frequently, for he can "make" your party. His subject is not important, it is the twist he gives to it, the personality he puts into it, that delights his listeners.

Tips for Conversing with Ease

- Take a risk —be the first to say hello. "Hello, I'm Michael Tomsic. My brother is on this team. Do you know any of the lacrosse players on this team?"
- Focus on your immediate environment. "What a fun pool party. How do you know Clara?"
- Be yourself.
- Balance the conversation – talking and listening.
- Seek out common interests and experiences.
- Ask easy to answer questions about the other person that let him know you want to get to know him. "Do you go to the Asheville School?", "What's your favorite sport?" or "How many brothers and sisters do you have?"
- Ask open ended questions. These questions usually begin with words like How? Why? In what way? How did you get involved? For example, "How long have you been taking guitar lessons?"
- Answer a question with more than two words. "I've been taking guitar for two years. I hope to play in a band at school this year." Don't simply say "Two years."

Tips for Improving your Conversations

- Be the first to say hello.
- Introduce yourself to others.
- Display your sense of humor. (If you don't have one, try to develop one).
- Be receptive to new ideas.
- Make an extra effort to remember people's names.
- Ask a person's name if you have forgotten it.
- Show curiosity and interest in others.
- Be a good listener. The best conversationalists often talk the least and listen the most.

Handling "Sore" Subjects with Care

Tactful people keep their prejudices to themselves. A tactful person involved in a discussion says "It seems to me," not "That is not so" which is tantamount to calling the other a liar.

If you find another's opinion totally unacceptable, try to change the subject as soon as possible. If you care too intensely about a subject, it is dangerous to allow yourself to say anything. That is, if you can only expound your own fixed point of view, then you should never mention the subject except as a platform speaker. But if, on the other hand, you are able to listen with an open mind, you may safely speak on any topic. After all, any mutually interesting topic may lead to one about which you don't agree. Then take care. It's much better to withdraw unless you can argue without bitterness or bigotry. Arguments between coolheaded, skillful opponents may be an amusing game, but it can be very, very dangerous for those who become hotheaded and ill-tempered.

The Tactless Blunder

It's like rubbing salt into an open wound to make such remarks as "What happened to Bobby's complexion since he went away to school?" or "Are your parents really getting a divorce?" or even "What's the matter with your baby brother?" when the child is handicapped. These questions may sound unbelievable but they, and worse, are constantly being asked by people who should know better.

If you have any sense, you won't talk to your grandmother about how you dread getting old, to a handicapped person about what fun skating is, or to a city dweller about your thriving garden.

It is not only unkind to ridicule or criticize others, but the tables can well be turned on those who do. A young girl asked a boy she hoped to date, "How can you possibly go out with *that* drip?" "Because," he replied, "she's my sister!"

Unpleasant Types to Avoid When Possible

The Bore	The Contradictor	The Secret-Teller
The Wailer	The Shifty Eye	Mr. Negative
The Sentence-Finisher		The Story Snatcher

How to Handle Snoopers

How do you answer personal questions about the cost of a gift, an item of clothing or a purchase you have made? You are under no obligation to give out this sort of information if you do not wish to. You can simply say "I don't know (or remember) what it costs." Or, if you wish to play up the value of the article, say "More than I probably should have paid," and if you wish to play it down, "Not as much as you'd think."

Inquiries about money matters are usually in poor taste and should be given short shrift. You cannot quite say, "None of your business," but you can say, "I'd rather not talk about that, if you don't mind," and change the subject.

Those Who Make Personal Remarks

Compliments and other favorable personal remarks are not only permissible but desirable. But unpleasant remarks, or bad remarks that make another person uncomfortable, are definitely in bad taste. The old adage, "If you can't say something nice, don't say anything at all" is very good advice.

There are occasions, however, when one wonders whether or not to make what might be construed as a critical remark. This might occur, for example, when you don't know whether you should tell your friend that he has a stain on his shirt. The answer depends on whether he can correct the situation or not. If there is a place where he can wash off the stain, by all means tell him. If not, calling attention to his problem will only make him self-conscious and aware of a fault of which he might otherwise have been unaware, or at least have thought was unnoticed.

People frequently wonder whether they should call an unzipped fly to the wearer's attention. Unless you are total strangers, do. The slight embarrassment to you and the other person at the time is nothing compared to the mortification he will feel when he discovers the condition and wonders how long it existed. If, however, you have just been introduced, leave it to someone who knows him better.

Corrections

When a person pronounces a word incorrectly, or makes a grammatical blunder, should you correct the error or should you repeat the error to avoid making the speaker uncomfortable?

Two wrongs don't make a right. Don't correct him or her, but when the opportunity arises, use the same word or phrase *correctly* and hope that the mistake will be recognized.

Grammatical Blunders

Much has been written and could be argued about grammar, pronunciation of words, slang expressions, speaking skills, etc. but this is not often a safe place to tread. It is easy for even some of the most educated people to fall into the use of grammatical blunders such as, "Where's it at?" "Irregardless," or "Me and my brother."

Not everyone is raised with the early advantages that teach good English (even though many a person may think they have been). There is no better way to cultivate taste in words than by constantly reading books of proven literary standing. In addition, there is no better way to cultivate good pronunciation and grammar — apart from association with cultivated and educated people — than by having a good dictionary and using it.

Ending a Conversation

What do you do after a conversational subject has been exhausted? Don't wait until you or your partner feels the tension and becomes bored or uncomfortable trying to think of something else to talk about. Abruptly walking away or disappearing is also not a positive end to a conversation. The best time to end a conversation is when you have both expressed yourselves and when the time seems appropriate to part ways. Ending a conversation in a warm and personable manner will leave both of you feeling good about the encounter.

It is best not to try to escape by saying, "Excuse me, I need to go to the restroom," unless you are truly going to the restroom. Chances are you'll be caught if you don't go where you've said you're going. A polite way to end the conversation is to sum up the conversation you've had, shake hands and move on. For example, "Joe, I have enjoyed hearing about your trip out west last summer. Thanks for sharing your adventure with me. Take care and I hope to get to see your photographs soon."

Compliments

We all love to receive compliments and tend to love those who offer them. Giving compliments to others is a friendly way to begin a conversation and to promote goodwill. Compliments make others feel good. Give them whenever you honestly can. One rule is that the compliment must be sincere. You can compliment others directly, indirectly, privately and in front of others. The next time you have a nice thought about someone, tell him or her. If we all did it more frequently, the world would be a happier place. The following tips will make you an expert in complimenting others:

- Compliment with sincerity and be careful not to gush. If you like a person's sweater, simply tell them with a phrase like, "What a handsome sweater." Avoid going on and on about the style, color, weave, etc. Adding a comment like "That sweater is better than the red one you wore yesterday," detracts from the compliment.

- Indirect compliments are compliments that let the other person know that you admire or value something about him or her without directly saying so. An opportunity to give indirect compliments often arises when you want assistance. For example, "This sweater is bulkier than ones I usually wear. You know so much about fashion, I'd really appreciate your opinion." Secondhand compliments are also an indirect way of making others feel good. For example, "Spencer told me that your serve was awesome on the tennis court yesterday."

- Giving compliments in the presence of others must be done with sensitivity to others who are present. Avoid giving a compliment to one person that might be interpreted as an insult to the others. For example, if you tell one person what a nice sweater he/she is wearing, the others present and wearing sweaters might feel that you are implying that you don't like theirs.

Receiving compliments can sometimes be like receiving a gift and deserve no less. Always let the giver know that you appreciate the gift of a compliment. In the United States it is appropriate to say "Thank you," "I'm glad you like it," "What a nice thing to say," or "I appreciate that." Responding to a compliment by denying it with a remark such as "This faded sweater is an old hand-me-down that has a hole under the arm, etc." is rude and may make the compliment giver feel that you don't respect or value his opinion. Europeans receive compliments without words by giving a friendly smile. Asians acknowledge with a gracious bow. As you can see, the universal etiquette custom of receiving compliments is to return a compliment of goodwill with a gesture of gracious appreciation.

Dance Etiquette

It's hard to describe the impact that dancing can have on your life. It's like opening a door to another sense or feeling. Some people feel awkward trying it, just like when learning anything new for the first time. But don't let that stop you. Take a chance and learn to dance. You won't regret it.

Dancing is a skill you can learn with lessons if it does not come naturally to you. The main purpose of dancing is to enjoy the companionship of others and to have fun moving around with a partner to the beat of music. This fun activity has a few rules which will make you feel comfortable on the dance floor if you know them.

First, there are a few manners to remember when you are attending dancing lessons. When you enter a ballroom for your classes you may be asked to enter in what is called the escort position. You have probably observed this when attending weddings where groomsmen escorted women to their seats.

To take the escort position, the man bends his right arm at the elbow and makes a fist, placing the fist right below the rib cage. He should stand very straight and tall. His partner should place her fingertips lightly on his forearm. She does not grab his arm tightly or use him as total support. The class teacher may assign you a partner or you may be given an opportunity to ask someone to dance.

Never decline a dance with a false excuse and then accept when someone you like better comes along. That will hurt the feelings of the first person. If you tell someone you are going for refreshments or to the restroom, then go.

Never roll you eyes or laugh when someone asks you to dance — always be considerate of the other person's feelings. And remember that it is perfectly acceptable for girls to ask boys to dance, too!

If you aren't comfortable with the dance steps, be honest with your partner. Perhaps he or she can help you. Simply say, "Excuse me" if you step on your partner's feet.

After dancing with a girl, it is polite for the man to say to his partner, "Thank you." The polite response from the woman is "I enjoyed it too" or something else such as "It was fun" or "It was a pleasure." However, girls do not traditionally thank men for a dance.

Formal Dances

A gentleman who escorts a lady to a dance or prom is expected to send her flowers on the day of the dance. Some men prefer to present the flower to the woman when they call for her. The flowers may be a small bouquet or a corsage which may be worn by the woman on the dress or wrist.

It is good manners for him to telephone her ahead of time to find out what she is wearing so he can order flowers that will complement her outfit. (Flowers are not expected to be sent before a simple, informal dance.) The woman is expected to wear the flower either on her dress, wrist or purse. It is traditional for the woman to also present the man with a boutonniere (a small flower worn in the man's lapel), when he arrives to pick her up for the dance.

A man who drives to pick up his date should get out of the car and walk to the woman's door. Never blow your horn or ask her to wait outside for you when you plan to pick her up! Greet her family, help her with her coat if she has one, walk with her to the car, open the car door for her and help her in and out of the car. At the end of the evening, help her in and out of the car and walk her to her door.

As previously mentioned, the first responsibility of guests at every dance or party after they have checked their coats is to go together to find the host and hostess of the party and greet them. At the end of the party, guests should find their hosts again and thank them for the party. The "plus one" rule is to add one special comment about the evening to the thank you. Greeting hosts at the beginning of the party and saying thank you before leaving the party are important courtesies that should never be overlooked.

The man who has asked a woman to a dance should always dance the first dance with the woman he invited to the party. He may dance with other women at the party so long as the woman he invited has a partner. If the man's partner is invited to dance with another man, he may choose to find a partner or "cut in" on a couple who is dancing. If she has no other partner to dance with, he should not abandon her completely to dance with others.

Cutting In

Men "cut in" by tapping the arm of the girl's partner. The man being tapped should step aside and allow the man cutting in to dance with his partner. When the person being tapped is dancing with the girl for the first time during the evening, he may smile and say "Next time around." If he does this, he must allow the man trying to cut in to dance with his partner the next dance. The girl always says, "I'm sorry" or something similar when leaving one partner for another partner. It is good manners for her not to show preference for one man over another as they have each paid her a compliment by asking her to dance. Male guests at a party should try to dance with the hostess of a party.

How to Ask Someone to Dance

The young man walks up to the woman of his choice. He _does not_ scrutinize each young woman at the dance before making his decisions. If he does not know the girl, he introduces himself to her and asks if she would care to dance saying, "May I have this dance?" If the girl does not know him she introduces herself. The girl accepts the dance by saying, "Yes, thank you." If the girl is standing, the boy offers her his arm and escorts her onto the dance floor. If she is seated, he should extend his left hand palm up. She accepts his hand with her right hand palm facing down and he gently helps her rise. Again, he offers her his right arm and escorts her onto the dance floor.

Remember, a dance is just a dance – not a commitment for life! If someone asks you to dance it is a compliment. Accept if at all possible. It takes courage to ask someone to dance and no one likes rejection. After all, a dance doesn't usually last more than three to five minutes. So go for it and have fun!

(I hope you dance!!!)

THE GOOD HOST

Friends and acquaintances will enjoy visits with you if you know how to be a good host. The following steps can make you a good host and your home a favorite place for friends to visit.

Extend an invitation to your guest to visit. Make clear the beginning and ending time of the invitation. Let your guest know if the invitation includes any special activity requiring special clothing (swimming, snow skiing, etc.)

Prepare for your guest. Make the environment one in which positive interaction can take place. Put away any objects that you do not want others to touch. Prepare for overnight guests by putting clean sheets on the bed and placing clean linen in the bathroom. Plan and prepare refreshments for your guests.

Plan activities for you and your guest. Have a few activities in mind and let your guest choose. Choose something in which two people can participate. It's not much fun watching one person play computer games meant for one person. Avoid activities that prevent you and your guest from enjoying each other. TV and video games are for times when you are alone. (Exception, extended guest visits may welcome a break).

Make your guest feel welcome. A host's number one priority is the comfort of his guest. Always greet your guest at the door. Smile and say "Thank you for coming!" Take the person's coat, backpack or other belongings. Introduce a new friend to your family. Old friends should greet your family too. Offer something to eat or drink. Even if you're not hungry or thirsty, your guest might be. The good host puts his guest's wishes before his own. Remember: The guest is always right, gets to choose the activities and is served the first and biggest piece of pie!

Be loyal to your guest. Never leave your guest alone for long unless your guest has come for an extended visit for several days and you both may crave some private time. If someone calls for you, politely tell them that you have company and tell them you will call them back later. Talking on lengthy phone conversations is rude. Walk your guest to the door and say good-bye when he leaves. If your parents are driving your guest home, you should ride along too and thank him or her for coming when they depart.

And finally, never criticize your guest. Make sure they have a good time, are comfortable in your house and want to return.

The Good House Guest

The welcome house guest is, above all else, adaptable. You must always be ready for anything – or nothing. If the plan is to picnic, you like picnics above everything and prove it by enthusiastically making the sandwiches or the salad dressing or whatever you do best. If, on the other hand, no one seems to want to do anything, find a book to absorb you, a crossword puzzle or walk on the beach by yourself.

Whether easy or not, you must conform to the habits of the family with whom you are staying. You take your meals at their hours, you eat what is put before you and you get up and go out and come in and go to bed according to the schedule arranged by your hostess. And no matter how much the hours or the food or the arrangements may upset you, you try to appear blissfully content. When the visit is over, you need never enter that house again, but while you are there, you must at least act as though you are enjoying yourself. You will be a popular guest if you follow the steps of a good house guest.

- *Arrive and depart on time.*
- *Wear and/or pack appropriate clothing* — pack for the unexpected. Rain gear or a coat and tie may be needed on any occasion.
- *Respect the rules of the house* — If breakfast is served at 7:00 a.m., be dressed and at the table at 7:00 a.m. Go to bed when your host signals. Be gracious and helpful at all times. Help clear your place at the table and put dishes into the dishwasher.
- *Never criticize your host.*
- *Be loyal to your host.*
- *Be tidy* — Leave any area you spend time in as nice, or nicer, than you found it. Make your bed daily (the correct way) and pick up your room. (If you don't know the correct way to make a bed, ask someone who does to show you.) Be particularly careful to keep your bathroom immaculate, especially if you are sharing it with others. Don't leave a ring in the tub, dried shaving residue in the sink, hairs any place or dirt on the soap. Hang up used towels. Flush. Place books or games back on the shelf. Turn off the lights. Close the doors. Offer to help in the kitchen preparing meals or cleaning up after the meal. Don't be nosy and wander into various rooms of the house or open drawers or closets. Don't read mail or notes that are lying out.
- *Be a conversation pro* — Remember that the best conversationalists often talk the least and listen most. Ask your host before using the telephone and avoid tying up the phone for long and making long distance calls charged to your host.
- *Express thanks* — Thank your host for his hospitality before you leave. Overnight visits require written thank you notes to the

host and/or his parents within a few days of your departure. The only exceptions are when your hosts are relatives or close friends with whom you visit back and forth frequently, or they are friends or neighbors with whom you travel regularly to their vacation home and back. Even then, a call the next day to say what fun you had would still be greatly appreciated. It is not only courteous, but obligatory to give your hostess a gift if you have come or been for an overnight visit. When you take a gift with you, give it to your hostess as soon as you arrive. If you send it later, it should be done as soon as possible. (In this case the hostess must write you *her* thanks — unless she lives next door and calls or runs over to thank you when the gift is delivered.)

- *Examples of gifts for a weekend visit*- include the conventional list of flowers, fruit, food or a book but be sure you know what kind of book she would like, that she is not on a special diet or that she has no flowers of her own in her garden or fruit on her trees. Some people prefer to send a present after their visit (having seen what the hosts might need or like) but if you don't plan to do that, you should arrive with an inexpensive gift to be used during your stay — a bottle of wine for the hosts, some homemade bread, a jar of special jam or a pretty potted plant. If you've checked with your hostess in advance you might bring some food or a casserole for dinner ready for heating. If your host and hostess have children, perhaps bring toys or a new game or puzzle the children could play together.

- *Be helpful upon your departure* — The morning of the day you are going to leave, ask your hostess what she would like you to do with your bed linen. She will probably say, "Oh just leave the beds," but don't! Unless she especially says, "The housekeeper is coming in later to make up the beds," then remove the sheets, fold them and pull the blanket and spread up neatly so that the bed will look made. If you make it up with your sheets in place, it is all too easy for a busy hostess to forget and then turn down the bed for the next guest, only to find the dirty sheets still on. Or, if you take her at her word and leave the bed untouched she is almost forced to do something about it after you leave, when she might rather be doing something else. If you are very close friends and a frequent visitor, make the bed up for her with fresh sheets yourself.

TELEPHONE SKILLS

When you talk on the telephone, whether at home, school or work, the quality of your conversation and your ability to express yourself clearly, politely and enthusiastically are important. They quickly tell the caller something about you — so be careful. You never know if the caller is someone trying to sell you something or calling to offer you a job!

Answering the Telephone
- Say, "Hello." The right way to answer a telephone in the home is to simply say "hello." It is not necessary to identify yourself or give your number for security reasons. Wait for the caller to identify himself before supplying your name, number, address or other information.
- Say, "This is he" or "This is Chris McMurry" if the call is for you.
- Say, "Please hold," or "Just a minute," when the caller asks to speak to someone in your home or nearby. If the call is for another member of the family, ask" May I ask who's calling?" or "May I tell my mother who's calling?" **not** "Who is this?
- Place the receiver on the table quietly when the phone is for someone else. Take the phone away from your mouth before calling in a medium-toned voice for the person. Inform the person being called by walking into the room where they are. Avoid covering the mouthpiece and yelling since much of what you say can be overheard — even when you think it cannot. Say something like "Hanna, you have a phone call." Do **not** yell "Hanna, a boy is on the phone for you" or "Mom, it's that woman who talks too much on the phone for you!"
- If the call is for someone who is not home or who cannot come to the phone, say, "My mother can't come to the phone right now. May I take a message?" **not** "My parents are away for the

evening," and **certainly not** "My mother is in the bathroom, can she call you back?" That is an example of **TMI** – Too much information!

Making a Telephone Call

- Identify yourself and state the reason for your call. "Hello. This is Simms Davenport. May I please speak to Thomas?" **Not**, "Is Thomas there?" When Thomas *does* answer your call, do ask if it is a convenient time to talk. If it is not, find out when you should call back.
- If the person you are calling isn't available, don't just hang up. It is correct to ask if the person will take a message such as, "Will you please tell him I called? I'm wondering if he can go to the lacrosse game this afternoon. Will you ask him to call me back?" Don't ask nosy questions such as, "Where is he?" or "Is he at Georgia's house?"
- Speak clearly. Avoid eating or chewing gum while talking.
- Keep the background noise in the area quiet. Loud radios and televisions can make conversations difficult.
- Focus your attention on the person to whom you are speaking. Speaking to others in the room with you should be avoided.
- Try to call, in most cases, between 9:00 a.m. and 9:00 p.m. Most families don't like to be disturbed during dinner or after 9:00 p.m. at night. Be considerate. If you are calling around the dinner hour, ask "Am I interrupting your dinner?" Calling before 9:00 a.m. on a weekend is not a good idea either.
- Keep calls brief. Telephone calls should rarely be longer than ten minutes. Remember that others may need to use the phone or those you are talking to might have other things to do. Ask if it is a convenient time to talk. "Is this a good time to talk?" or "Am I interrupting you?" "Do you have a minute to give me directions to the ski slopes?"
- Remember that it is the caller's responsibility to end the call.

Call Waiting

- Wait until a break in conversation before responding to the call-waiting signal. Courtesy to the first person you are on line with comes first. Then excuse yourself and say, "Please excuse me for just a moment," or "Can you hold for just a moment?"
- Switch to the second caller and say, "Hello" and wait for the caller to identify him/herself.
- If the call is for you, let the caller know immediately that you have someone on the other line and that you'll return the call in a few minutes. Then do so.
- If the call is for another person, give the message as soon as possible.
- If the call is for a parent or if the call is urgent and for another person, ask the second caller to hold and tell the first caller that you'll call them back later. Do so. Immediately summons the person for whom the urgent call was made.

Answering Machines

- The outgoing message on your machine should be brief. Few people have the time or the interest in listening to a lengthy message. Ten to fifteen seconds is an appropriate length. Do not try leave a personalized, humorous or tasteless message aimed at getting a laugh from the caller. You never know who the caller might be and they might be calling about something that is important to you. The first impression they get of you over the phone (in your message) could make the difference in how they react after hearing your message.
- Include a simple greeting such as "Hello, please leave your name, number and a message and I will return your call as soon as possible." It is not necessary to include instructions such as, "after the beep."
- Your name and number might give information to strangers which you could later regret.

Leaving a Message on Someone Else's Machine

- State your name, number and the purpose for your call.
- Remember that what you say on a machine might be heard by

many people. Avoid leaving a message that might embarrass others.

- Keep your message brief. A good, brief message with concise information might say," Hello, this is Frank Jackson calling for Stephen Covington. It's 10:30 Saturday morning. I have tickets to the UNC basketball game tonight and wonder if he'd like to go with my sister and me. Please call me as soon as possible. If I haven't heard from him by 2:00 p.m. I will assume he cannot go and will make other plans. Thanks very much. Bye."

How to Handle a Wrong Number

If you incorrectly dial a number simply say, "I'm sorry, I have the wrong number." If someone calls you by mistake say, "I'm sorry, there is no one here by that name."

When the caller asks, "What number is this?" or "Who is this?" you should reply, "What number did you call?" or "Who are you trying to call?" Never tell a stranger your name or phone number.

How to Take a Message

Have a pad of paper and a pencil or pen by the phone. Ask for the name of the caller and his phone number. Ask the person to spell his name if you don't know how. Carefully write the phone number and repeat it — "Let me repeat the number, 762-7228?" Leave the message in an agreed upon place- don't forget to let the person you took the message for know there was a call!"

Cell Phone Skills

- *Safety — Pay attention to the road.* Growing evidence shows that cell phones distract drivers and put others at risk. Never use a mobile phone while driving unless it is "hands free." Not only are both hands free to steer, but there seems to be significant improvement in attention deficit when using an ear phone. The ear phone makes it easier to focus on driving. Also, limit conversations in cars to traffic areas and conditions requiring low amounts of decision making. In high volume, tricky driving situations, either turn the phone off or let it ring.

- *Volume – Speak softly.* You should speak in hushed tones since a mobile phone has a sensitive microphone that can pick up a soft voice. Set the ring tone at a level that is soft, gentle and not annoying. Switch to vibrate mode in situations like a church or a meeting where a ringing sound would prove disturbing to other people. The idea is to try to gain as little phone attention as possible and the goal is to communicate effectively without anybody else noticing or caring.

- *Proximity – Keep your distance.* Each person is surrounded by a personal space which provides feelings of safety and calm, especially in crowded places. You should respect the personal space of others and try to speak in places 10-20 feet or more away from the closest person. Crowded rooms, lines and tight hallways are not good places to carry on a phone conversation. Sensitivity to other peoples' needs and comforts is a sign of good character.

- *Content – Keep business private.* Many personal and business conversations contain information that should remain confidential or private. Before using a mobile phone in a public location to discuss private business or issues you should make sure there is enough distance to keep the content private.

- *Tone – Keep a civil and pleasant tone.* Always know that others might overhear a conversation so be careful to maintain a public voice that will not disturb others. However, certain types of conversations may require or inspire some tough talk or emotional issues. Reserve these conversations for more private settings. Do not fire employees, chastise someone or argue with anyone in public settings.

- *Location – Pick your spot.* Some locations are better for conversations than others. They offer more privacy and less noise. By keeping your cell phone turned off much of the time, you can handle incoming calls under good conditions rather than struggling against interference of various kinds. Learn which spots will offer the best signal and the best conditions rather than hold an important discussion under poor conditions.

- *Timing – No cell phone before its time.* Think about when to turn the phone on or off. There are many situations where it would be rude if a phone rang, interrupting the transaction at hand. Stepping up to a service counter, sitting in a classroom, entering a restaurant or joining a meeting are times to turn off the phone or its ringer and rely upon voicemail to take incoming calls.

- *Multi-tasking — One thing at a time.* Some folks are better than others at juggling many tasks at the same time, but there are some things in life that deserve your full attention. Reserve multi-tasking for times when it is safe, convenient and appropriate. Approaching a counter to work through a problem with an airline ticket is a good time to turn your cell off to protect the coming transaction from interruption. One thing at a time. Focus. Efficiency. Manners.

Travel Etiquette

Current news abounds with stories about declining manners on board airplanes. Flight attendants and airline personnel have numerous stories of abusive, rude passengers. Likewise, travelers feel slighted by airline employees. Long lines, delayed flights, lost luggage, catering mistakes — all are compounded when crowds of people are in a hurry. Unfortunately, flight attendants endure most of the bad behavior. A few tips to follow:

- Avoid using loud, threatening or abusive language toward airline personnel.
- Remember that flight attendants are on board for your safety- they are not like waiters in a restaurant.
- Airlines are in the business of transporting you — not impressing you with fancy meals, snacks or beverages.
- Catering mistakes are not the fault of the flight attendants. This includes forgetting special meals, not having enough meals or serving meals you don't like, etc.
- Dress appropriately for being in public, in close quarters with others, and where you will leave a first impression on many people. It is fine to wear casual and comfortable clothes for

travel but dress appropriately. Sweatsuits, for example, may be comfortable but perhaps too casual. On the other hand, baring too much skin with tank tops or tube tops, low cut tops, mini-skirts or short shorts is inappropriate for both men and women. It is also hard to keep warm on an airplane when dressed in this manner.

- No one can control the weather – don't take out your frustrations about canceled flights on airline personnel.

Airlines have a limited amount of air space:

- Don't try to bypass luggage claim by toting all of your belongings on the plane and taking more than your share of overhead storage space.
- Avoid strolling down the narrow aisle with too many bags and banging into the other passengers with your bags.
- Stay in your "space" – don't spread your work across the seats or hold your newspaper in your seatmate's face.
- Adhere to airline rules regarding portable computer and cell phone usage.
- Avoid striking up long, personal conversations with the person sitting next to you. Exchange a few pleasantries, but don't continue to talk to someone if he is trying to work or relax.
- Leave the lavatory spotless. Use a paper towel to wipe around the sink- even if the person before you was the one who left it in a mess.
- Leave your seat area neat and clean. Properly dispose of napkins, cups, apple cores, newspapers and other papers.
- Say "Thank you" to the crew as you deplane.

FUNERALS

Every moment of your life will not be happy. Inevitably, people you know will get sick or struck by tragedy and some day die. Ignoring sickness, death and moments of sadness will not make them go away. However, knowing what to expect and how to respond during unhappy times will help you and those who need you.

Help the Grieving

Let those who are grieving know that you care about them and are sorry for their loss. It is painful to experience the death of someone special. Sadness can be compounded when others who care remain silent and do nothing. Not expressing sympathy may be interpreted by those who are mourning as a sign that no one cares. You can let those who are mourning know that you care in several ways.

Condolence Calls

When someone dies the feeling of loss is often overwhelming. Friends and family who rally around the grieving can be a big help. It is greatly appreciated if you can visit the grieving at their home. Your presence is a show of support and lets them know that they are not alone. Close friends often help in many ways such as answering the telephone and the door, preparing meals and keeping a written record of visitors and any food, flowers or gifts that are received. Sometimes the family prefers to see people at the funeral home or at the church. Look in the newspaper obituary for this information.

You will want to visit during the seven days after the funeral if your friend is Jewish and the custom of sitting shivah is practiced. (The time before the funeral is generally a time for family to be together.)

Listen to your grieving friend when he wants to talk. Being present when a grieving person needs to talk is important. It is not necessary for you to talk when your friend is trying to find or sort out answers. Being present to listen is what he needs from you. Be sincere when you speak and avoid clichés such as "He is at peace now," and references to religion that the bereaved may not share or appreciate. Say the deceased person's name and share memories. Repeating humorous stories about the deceased will often lighten the sadness.

Notes of Condolence

Letting those who are sad know that you care is very comforting. Many stores sell sympathy cards, but the most personal notes are those that are handwritten. The most traditional condolence notes are written in black ink on formal letter sheets. Write what you truly feel. Be sincere. Let the person know that you are sorry and that you care. Write about anything you remember about the person who died that made that person special or unique. Funny stories are okay, as in "I loved the way he always sang off key at the caroling parties." Avoid formal or flowery language or saying things like, "It was a blessing in disguise," "She wouldn't want you to cry and be sad," or other phrases that try to minimize the loss. The person you are comforting needs to know simply that you care. Therefore, it is not necessary to write a long note. Here is an example of a sympathy note:

Dear George,

I am so sorry to learn of your dad's death. He was one of my favorite people. I'll never forget the fun time he took us camping at Oyster Creek. He took us hunting, helped us build a huge bonfire afterward and then led us in singing around the campfire. I'll miss him. You and your family are in my thoughts and prayers. Please let me know if there is anything I can do.

Your friend,
Bill

Telephone Calls of Condolence
You may choose to telephone to express your sympathy. However, remember that visitors will likely be at the home immediately after the death and that it could be inconvenient to tie up the phone line. Close family members unable to attend the funeral will of course want to telephone right away. However, remember that it is often a better idea to wait until your friend can have an uninterrupted conversation with you when the home is not so busy.

Food and Flowers
Family and friends who have gathered appreciate food. If you are a close friend, you might consider preparing a dish for them and delivering to the home.

In the United States, it is a Christian custom to send flowers to the home of the deceased, the place of worship or the funeral home unless the obituary requests that no flowers be sent. Sign accompanying cards with your first and last names. If you learn of the death after the funeral, it is acceptable to send flowers late. In fact in the Islamic culture, flowers should be sent after the funeral. Be aware that some religions and cultures have customs regarding flowers. For example, in

France, chrysanthemums symbolize mourning and in Japan, the color white symbolizes death. Traditional Jewish custom views flowers as a joyful expression so it is preferable to express sympathy in other ways to those grieving families.

Donations to Charities
Sometimes the family prefers that no flowers be sent. This is indicated in the newspaper obituary or by the phrase "in lieu of flowers a donation may be sent to…" A donation in the approximate amount of an arrangement of flowers is appropriate. Send the donation directly to the designated charity (not to your friend) along with a note indicating the name of the person the gift is in memory of and the address of the bereaved so the family can be notified of your gift. Donations to other charities are appropriate, especially if a specific charity has not been designated for memorials.

Keep in Touch
After the funeral, your friend will continue to be sad. Demonstrate your support of your friend by periodically calling or visiting. The first anniversary of his loved one's death will be especially difficult as will be the first holidays without the special person. He will appreciate your kindness. Invite your friend out and offer to accompany him to the cemetery.

What to Do and Expect When Someone Close To You Dies
This will be one of the hardest events you will ever experience. No one can prepare you for the way you will feel. Everyone feels differently. Knowing that other people care will comfort you. You can expect family and friends to visit, telephone and to do nice things for you. Accept the love and support of other people that will not only help you but also helps them work through their own process of grieving. People will not expect you to carry on conversations or feel like doing many of the things you usually do. Participate as you feel you are able, and say "thank you" when others show kindness. Take care of yourself.

After the funeral or memorial service, you and your family will probably feel extremely tired and sad for a long time. It may take a long time for you to feel happy again. The length of time is different for everyone. Your family and friends will offer support but if your grief is overwhelming, you might want to get professional help or counseling.

Acknowledgements of Sympathy
When life begins to return to normal, one of the first things you will want to do is thank those who sent food, flowers, gave donations to charities, wrote personal notes of condolence or expressed their sympathy in other special ways. A simple thank you note from you or a close family member will be appreciated. The note need not be long, but it should be handwritten. Traditional thank you notes for a personal expression of sympathy are written on fold-over notes. Courtesy notes are often supplied by funeral homes but use personal fold-over notes if you have them or can get them. Engraved or printed cards are appropriate to send to acknowledge impersonal messages of sympathy which are too numerous to thank with a personal note. It is not necessary to write to those who sent sympathy cards with no personal message or to those who visited the funeral home.

Appropriate Clothing
Gone are the days when black clothing was the only acceptable color to be worn when mourning. However, subdued colors and clothing that does not attract attention is appropriate. Those in mourning generally receive many visitors who come to offer support and show respect. One way visitors show respect is by wearing nice clothing.

Those grieving need to dress accordingly to receive these visitors. Adults typically wear dark suits and dresses to funerals. Young children wear their best clothes.

References

McMurry, Jane Hight. The Dance Steps of Life. Wilmington: Stellar Publishing, 2002.

McMurry, Jane Hight. The Etiquette Advantage®. Wilmington: Stellar Publishing, 2002.

Phoneybusiness.com. "Etiquette." Online posting. Mobile Etiquette. 5 July 2005. <http://phoneybusiness.com/etiquette.html>.

Post, Elizabeth L. Emily Post's Etiquette. New York: Harper & Row, Publishers, 1984.

To Manner Born, To Manners Bred. Hampden-Sydney: Hampden-Sydney College Office of the Dean of Students, 2000.